Journey To The Heart
Through
The Way of the Horse

Sara B. Willerson

ISBN:099128870X
ISBN-13:9780991288700

DEDICATION

This book is dedicated to my beloved horse Pooh. Without him, none of this would be possible.

Cover Artwork by Rene Stigler

Author's photo by Teri Relyea Berbel

CONTENTS

Look deep into nature, and then you will understand everything
better.

- Albert Einstein

ACKNOWLEDGMENTS

This book has been a process of self discovery and incredible growth for me. It has taken years to gather my courage and put onto to paper what horses have been saying to me and urging me to share with humanity. So many people have been supportive of me and have not thought this was a totally crazy idea. They may not have totally understood this endeavor, but their love for both me and my passion for horses has been the underlying base and I could not have accomplished this without them.

For my parents, Nancy and Jim Willerson. I cannot express the depth of gratitude and love I have for you both. Throughout my life you have supported me personally, professionally, and at times, financially. You gave me the gift of horses in my life and have always supported my pursuit of creating this dream of a profession I now have. Thank you for believing in me and helping to make my dream turn into reality.

For my sister, Amy Willerson. You are an amazing person and I could not ask for a better sister. Thank you for cementing the deal on getting Pooh into my life. Thank you also for your beautiful children, Jimmy, Grace and Thomas and sharing the love of horses with them.

For all of my ancestors who had a special touch and relationship with animals. Thank you for passing this gift along and always watching over me.

For Brian, The Sweetest Man In The World. Thank you for loving me (even though you still think I'm weird) and being willing to step into my life with these amazing horses and beautiful land. I am so grateful you are in my world.

Christine Agro, came into my life almost six years ago when a friend shared a New York Times article about her animal communication gifts. I immediately contacted her to help me chat with my cat Louise. From there I have participated in many courses she has offered on consciousness, healing, and living life as Spirit. She has truly changed my world. Her support of me personally and professionally always brings tears to my eyes and I am so grateful we have crossed paths. And thank you for helping me edit and publish this book!!! Without you this would not be happening.

Other supporters of my business endeavor whom I am so thankful for and have learned much from include Mary Clark, Pancho (who always took such loving care of Pooh, Magno and Jingles), Nisse, Tammy and her family at Cypress Equestrian Center, Joe Lopez, Roseberry Farm (Jean and Jean Marie Dunford and Jim), The Monarch School, Angela Caughlin, Becky Joyce, Bo's Place, Boys and Girls Country, David Nixon (my favorite Guardian Angel Pastor), Quintes Stark, Shirley Wright, Stan Tubbs, Rhonda George, Vicki and Julia, Sharon Hibdon, Jennifer Watson, Katherine Mize, Betty and Bob Dicken, Christine Eger, Jean Sullivan, Vanessa Sanford , Ann Marie Warren, Karen Hutchins, Gerry Starnes, Jodi Roberts, Teri Relyea Berbel, Sean Mathis, Lance and Jeannette Wright, Margaret and Bill Couch, Tricia Hatle, Sandra Wallin, Laurel Boyer, the staff at UNT Counseling and Testing Center, Maryann Gerity, Molly Sweeney, Ken Baines, Jackie Doval, i360 Life, Caron Texas, Hope For Horses Equine Rescue, Paige Skonieczny, Ashley Gibson, Amy Sophiella, Divya Chandra, Mudita Chandra, Ali Shields, the Eponaquest Community, and of course, The Shawomen- you know who you are.

I am incredibly grateful for all the people who have come to work with me and the horses and have been open to healing in an entirely new way. Thank you for sharing your stories, your gifts and your healing. You all are profoundly inspirational for me.

And of course, for all the horses in my life: Spice, Duchess, Diamond, Annie, Pooh, Magno, Moonbeam, Jingles, Spirit, Asante, Thera, and Domino. And all of the other horses and horse ancestors I have had the privilege of learning from and with. You **all** have made me the person I am today and I constantly strive to live your way of being.

PROLOGUE

From the time I can remember horses have been a part of my life. The first time my grandfather put me on Spice the black and white paint pony, I knew I had found my passion. So after summer camps and weekly riding lessons for many years, I finally convinced my parents to get a horse.

The first horse in my life was not the perfect partner for me (she truly enjoyed bucking me off on a just about daily basis). She did teach me a lot about caring for a horse and my responsibility to another life other than my selfish 13 year old self. She also colicked on a pretty regular basis so I got really good at diagnosing that one too. But it was the day that I came home with black eyes after being bucked off for the gazillionith time, that my mom said, "That's enough" and I knew I was just given permission to find my perfect partner.

One day, my dedication to the classifieds was rewarded, I saw 'The Ad'. My Horse. He was listed as an 11 year old Quarter Horse/Arab gelding hunter/jumper. Without telling my parents, I called the listed number and talked to the owner of what I knew was my horse. I talked my cool babysitter Kate into taking me to see him. Only then did I inform my parents that I had found my horse and I was going to go and meet him.

I went to see my horse and I just knew. I knew when I saw the ad in the paper, but when we were together in person, I **really knew**, Heart and Soul, this horse and I were meant to be together. I rode him and felt as if I'd been riding him forever. I asked the owner his

1

name and she said Xanadu. Please keep in mind this was the early '80s. I just kind of stared at her because I couldn't imagine this horse as Xanadu. Then she said, "But I also call him Pooh sometimes." Pooh it was. My parents came to meet him and knew there was no way to change my mind or talk me out of this. It took some time for us to be together but eventually everything fell in place.

I was 14 and Pooh was 11 and we did everything together; jumping, swimming, bareback rides at a flat out run, naps on his back while he grazed, a little bit of showing here and there, and lots of quality time together. Every day after school I made a mad dash to be with him. Once I got to the barn, I'd call out Pooh's name and he'd call right back to me. He was my best friend, my confident, my strong understanding shoulder, my therapist and my protector. He ALWAYS understood me no matter what was going on and no matter what I walked into his presence with. Anything I asked of him, he would do. One day my riding instructor said, "Sara, you trust that horse too much." To me that was a compliment because I knew I could and that was the relationship we had. Coming from her, she had no clue about this relationship between me and Pooh. This was also a very clear reminder to me that most people had no conscious awareness of the magical 'beingness' of horses.

Pooh was with me through high school and he was a great support during my turbulent teen years. When it was time for college, I chose Hollins, a women's college in Virginia, partly because it had a riding program. It was difficult to leave Pooh in Texas but I would see him during breaks and over the summer. During that first summer break, in a great moment of synchronicity, the owners of Roseberry Farm, where Pooh was living in Texas, decided to relocate to Virginia and offered to bring Pooh with them. This presented the opportunity to have Pooh join me at school. I contacted the college and they had an open stall for him. Pooh's sophomore year enrollment was complete. The college placement wasn't the best home for Pooh (very little turnout and he was getting very grumpy with no outside time) so I moved him back to Roseberry Farm. As time moved on, our visits turned to weekends. No matter how long it had been in between visits , he always called out to me upon my arrival.

I got married and returned to Texas in the fall of 1998 and was finally going to be in one place for a stable period of time. I arranged the transportation and at 25 years old Pooh joined me again. After all the years of him caring and watching over me, it was now my turn to give back to him. We didn't do much riding, but we continued to spend lots of time with each other.

When the year 2000 rolled around, I sensed that Pooh was beginning to think about completing this lifetime. I knew that my heart could not handle losing him without another horse present. I came across a website called DreamHorse.com and started looking around. I had become drawn to Andalusians and in no time found one for sale in Austin. He was a three year old Andalusian/Percheron mix. The pictures the owner had posted were not the prettiest but something deep inside told me said that this horse, named Magno, and I were supposed to be together. I contacted the owner and she said that another person was very interested in him and coming to see him the next day. I asked her to keep me posted and that night I prayed many prayers that the prospective buyer would not want him after all. The next day I received an email from the owner saying the woman had decided to buy a trailer instead. I quickly responded that I would drive down the next day to meet Magno. I sped down to Austin with my trainer and when Magno's owner introduced us, I started laughing. I am five foot in height and was introduced to this massive mix of Percheron and Andalusian whose head was as big as my head and torso combined. He looked at me from his stall door and dropped his head into my arms. I was done. Here was the newest member of our herd. He didn't have much training yet but I knew that we would be learning a lot with each other. Magno came down to Houston about a week later and he and Pooh became friends immediately.

2000 was becoming a year of great change. As Pooh worked his way through his transition, it also became clear to me that my marriage was coming to an end. Pooh and Magno were my place of serenity during this time. My divorce became final at the end of 2001 and several days after that I found myself sitting on the back porch of my about to be sold house with my cat Louise winding through my legs. I experienced only what I can describe as a download of light coming into the top of my head that completely woke me up. I became very aware of how asleep and disconnected I had been from myself and realized it was time to wake up. I would sit with Pooh in his pasture and just hear him tell me, "Don't worry, everything is going to be ok. Just wait and see." I could see the gleam in his eyes as he shared his wisdom with me and I decided to trust his words.

Pooh's wisdom became clear when my father gave me the book, *The Tao of Equus*, by Linda Kohanov as a Christmas present that year. I'm not sure he knew what he was giving me. He loves to give books as gifts and I think he probably saw the picture of a horse on the cover and thought I'd enjoy it. *The Tao of Equus* changed my life forever. The author put words and meaning to every experience I had ever had with my equine friend. I could not stop crying as I read this book. Kohanov wrote about human healing through interactions with horses and put forward the theory that horses are sentient beings who have amazing healing gifts to share with humans. As I read Kohanov's theory, I had my own awakening.

I now had a Masters in Social Work and was working toward my licensure to be a private practice therapist. The idea that I could combine my love of working with people in their healing process with my passion for horses was amazing. It was like the light finally got turned on inside of me and I felt alive like never before. I immediately went to the author's website and signed up for a workshop at The Epona Center (now known as Eponaquest). This particular workshop offered an experiential introduction to the program they were developing. I knew my life was about to take a very different path from a traditional 9-5 practice. It was kind of scary but absolutely what I was being called to do. I was very clear about that for the first time in my life. Pooh had been preparing me for this journey and although I did not know how it was all going to unfold, I trusted this was my path to follow.

Several months after attending this workshop, I received an email from Eponaquest saying they were starting an apprenticeship program. Again I had the reaction of feeling that total energetic download experience. I knew I had to apply. I put all the paperwork together in record time and overnighted it to Eponaquest in Arizona. I received the acceptance letter dated on my birthday in 2002. For me, yet another wonderful symbol that I was on the right path.

During my apprenticeship year, I started having vivid dreams in which I let go of "the day job" and moved into equine facilitated psychotherapy practice full time. These dreams were exciting and terrifying all at the same time. When I woke up I found myself thinking, what if it didn't work out, how would I guarantee I could pay the bills and who would really want to pay to do this work?

I passed my social work licensing exam and my dreams intensified and became more pressing. I finally decided to take a deep breath and trust what was supposed to happen. Besides, I really needed to get some sleep! So even through all the looks of concern and non-verbals I was getting from family and friends, I went to my supervisor at the grief support center where I worked, and shared the news. I gave a month's notice and I madly started sending out brochures to anyone and everyone I had ever met in the Houston therapeutic world. Slowly but surely I was getting responses and promises of client referrals. The staff at the barn where Pooh and Magno lived even worked overtime to help me get the word out about my new business, Horses, Heart & Soul, LLC. Everyday I'd go sit with Pooh and he continued to tell me, "Don't worry. It's all going to work out."

One day my financial prayers were answered. I received a call from the director of a children's residential home that was around the corner from Pooh and Magno's barn. She and I had worked together several years before and I had sent her a brochure because they had horses on their property for the kids to ride. She told me they hadn't done anything with the horses in a couple of years and as the kids were writing their goals for the summer, many of them requested to ride the horses. She told me she received my brochure the following day and "knew it was meant to be." Here was the stable financial piece I had been praying for. They wanted me to create a therapeutic equine program with the kids and their 11 horses plus manage the care of this special herd. And it was 15 minutes around the corner from Pooh and Magno so I could easily see private practice clients in addition to this position. The perfect plan had just presented itself.

Pooh became the leader in my private therapy practice work with children and adults. No matter the client's age or area of focus, he was right there with them, assisting their healing process and helping them make connections in their lives. Everyone loved Pooh. He was 30 at this point and starting to slow down physically. However, he remained very clear that his purpose was to continue helping people heal. Whoever he was working with, I would watch him look deep into that person's eyes, help them find the deep wound, and release it from their physical space. He was also very clear he was still helping me heal.

Given his physical state, I requested to change his turnout company. My younger horse Magno was 7 years old and a bit too much energy for Pooh. There was a spunky pony owned by the boarding barn named Jingles who was Pooh's age and Jingles didn't have a pasture mate. I was given permission to turn Jingles out with Pooh and they became best friends. We all jokingly called them The Grumpy Old Men Club as they were always very clear about how they felt about an issue and had no trouble stating what they wanted when they wanted it. As Pooh and I continued to work with clients, Jingles began to participate as well and became part of the treatment team. Jingles, like Pooh, had that ability to connect with a person heart and soul and help them see patterns in their life that were no longer working and find ways to transition to a life affirming flow. All of this happened for the person so simply; through a hand on the horse's side, by brushing them or just leading them around the stable. Especially with the children's programs, these two distinguished gentlemen always knew exactly what each child needed and helped them to feel safe and loved. It was a beautiful process to witness.

In the summer of 2005, it became clear that Pooh would not be with us much longer. Physically he had really slowed down and at 32, things just weren't working as well as they used to. Pooh was pretty clear he still had some important things to do before it was time to go. Not only did he guide me into this work and serve as a co-therapist for many people's healing, he also gave my 2 year old nephew Jimmy his first ride on a horse. He opened my heart to the possibility of loving and trusting again. He brought many people together. It didn't matter who you were or what your background was – you could look into Pooh's warm, loving eyes and stand in his generous compassionate presence and know that everything was going to be ok. Even someone who came to help him feel better always left feeling like they were the one who received the healing. Ken Baines, a friend of mine who is an animal massage therapist, came out to give Pooh a massage one day to help relax his tight muscles. When he was finished, Ken had tears in his eyes and said, "I don't how that horse does it but I think he just made me feel better instead of the other way around."

The day came that I knew he was ready to go. I looked into his eyes and I knew. I had tried to give him his pain medication that evening and he held it in his mouth, looked me straight in the eye and then spit it out on the ground. I knew he was telling me he was ready to go. I knew how he wanted this transition to be and I made the arrangements for the next day. I knew where he wanted to be buried

– under his favorite tree on the hill in his old pasture. Our barn graciously allowed all of this process to occur and they even closed the facility to ensure privacy. Pancho, who fed Pooh and turned him out, informed me that he would spend that last night outside Pooh's stall and watch over him. He made me go home and told me I needed to get a good night's sleep. I returned the next morning and I spent a long time with Pooh, Jingles and Magno.

While I was with Pooh in his stall, Pancho and all the other grooms began to bring just about every horse on the property to Pooh's stall to tell him goodbye. It was indescribable to watch these animals touch noses with Pooh and one by one, communicate their thoughts and sentiments across a few breaths. Pooh and each horse visitor would look at each other, touch noses, close their eyes partly and breathe together for a few breaths. It was as if time paused for several moments and all became quiet as they shared their thoughts and wisdom with each other. Then quietly the visitor stepped away in almost a reverent manner.

The vet had arrived and I led Pooh out of his stall and past Magno to begin our walk to his resting place. As we walked past Magno, he lunged at me with his teeth bared and stopped just short of biting me. I looked him and understood all of his anger, fear, sadness and his sense of the unknown. I told Magno, "It's not my fault! He is ready to go." I then watched as Pooh turned to Magno and shared a moment of breath with him. I saw Magno become calm and understand that his friend was ready to go.

When the vet arrived we began to walk toward Pooh's favorite tree in his pasture. The property was veiled in silence – even the birds had ceased singing. With my mother and sister by my side, I said the words I wanted to say and looked deep into my friend's soulful eyes. We had spent more than 20 years together. Even though I knew he would no longer be with me physically, I knew he would always be with me in Spirit.

The time came for him to go and I held him until long after his soul had been released. Pancho led Magno and Jingles up to the tree so they could see he was gone and say their final goodbyes. Magno was very quiet now and understood his friend had returned to his Spirit form. Jingles was a bit antsy and danced around a bit around his friend's physical form as if to say, "I already know he is gone. Why do I have to do this?" Pancho then led the horses back to their stalls and I watched Pancho talking and stroking them both reassuringly as they walked.

I stayed with Pooh as he was buried and Pancho made sure that Pooh was arranged comfortably in his resting place. I lay on top of his grave for a long time after the burial was complete and listened to the silence. Then out of nowhere, hundreds of dragonflies showed up and hovered around the grave for a good long while. Ted Andrew's book *Animal Speak*, which shares the symbolism of animals, is a personal favorite of mine. I looked up the meaning of dragonfly and saw that they assist a being in the transition between life and death. It was such a beautiful visual reminder.

It has been eight years since Pooh's death. I know he has been with me in spirit throughout all this time. I know he has continued to be a guide in my life throughout the development of my passion and purpose. I know he was part of the process of finding WolfTree Ranch, the special land where seven horses, two dogs, four cats and I have created a conscious space for healing. I feel him looking over my shoulder and I feel his warm, loving presence every day. I am so grateful to have shared time with such an amazing being. I am so grateful to him for being with me, for teaching me, guiding me and helping me to be the person I was meant to be. Pooh opened the door and reminded me of my ability to hear the messages the horses have to share. His presence has truly been such a gift and I will cherish him always.

It is to Pooh that this book is dedicated.

PHOTO BY MARYANN GERITY

INTRODUCTION

The impetus for this book came about six years ago during a journey I experienced with my Shamanic Group in Austin. In this journey, I found myself surrounded by horses as far as I could see. Thousands upon thousands of horses were around me. They had come, they said, to ask me to write their story. To write about their way, The Way of the Horse. At the time, I was terrified.

Who was I to write such an epic? Why did they want me to do this? I kept this Shamanic experience in the back of my head for a long time due to fear and lack of confidence in myself. Then I started having dreams with all the horses visiting me. Pushing and prodding me to do this. This experience spilled over with my current horses; Magno, Jingles and a mare called Moonbeam. Every time I went out to be with them, even when I was feeding them breakfast, they would look at me and say, "It's time to write the book. When are you going to get started?!" Moonbeam, who was the lead horse of this herd, was especially, let's call it **direct,** about getting the point across. Mares have an innate ability to make themselves known and heard through very clear facial expressions and body language...some of them not always so pleasant!

So I slowly began writing. Every couple of months I felt guided to sit down and write what the horses in my life had to say. I am excited to share their wisdom in this book for it is vast and truly powerful. I also found myself guided to sit with other horses and write down what they had to share. Another push to continue writing came in the summer of 2010. I received a notification from The Kentucky Horse Park (KHP) about a special, once in a lifetime exhibit they were creating called "A Gift from the Desert." This exhibit was dedicated to the Arabian horse. It was a gathering of very ancient artifacts from personal collections from around the globe, in addition to telling the story of the Arabian horse. Since Moonbeam is half Arabian, I knew this was a sign I could not ignore. Once again I felt that pulling in my soul that I had to go to this exhibit.

This exhibit detailed the history and sacredness of the Arabian horse throughout several cultures. I moved through this exhibit almost as if in a dream. This magical forbearer of all horses, The Arabian, had so many powerful messages. I was surrounded by texts and messages that spoke of the sacredness of the Arabian horse. What became clear to me was that The Arabian truly was a gift from God or Spirit. I became acutely aware that their presence is no coincidence and there is a clear meaning and reason for their being on this earth.

I had been to the KHP several years prior to attend the Rolex Three Day Event. This is an amazing competition and partnership of horse and rider. These special duos are required to compete in Dressage, Cross Country jumping, and Stadium Jumping events over the course of three days. This event is a world qualifying competition and this particular one was occurring before the next Olympics so I went to watch.

What I witnessed during the Rolex event, blew me away. The hearts and energy coming off of these horses was something I had only experienced with Pooh. While I was there, I madly wrote down the physical, emotional and spiritual information that surrounded me. An example I can give occurred on the cross country course. I had a close up view at several of the massive obstacles that horse and rider were asked to jump. As the partners came toward the jumps, I felt immeasurable amounts of energy preceding them as they approached. I felt my heart expand to a size I had only felt around Pooh when we were in that place of total connection and trust. I knew this was the connection of hearts between the two beings, in partnership together.

I was aware of such tremendous love energy that existed in this moment of horse and rider moving in totally harmony together. I understood this was the heart energy of love in its pure Spirit essence. It blew me away and tears streamed down my face.

I knew there was something very important about all of this. During a break in the competition, I went to the Museum of The Horse, located on the KHP grounds. This is an incredible exhibit detailing the history of the horse. As I wandered through the exhibit, I found myself getting inundated with messages from all of these ancient equine ancestors. So much information was coming, it was difficult to keep up with all the words swirling around me. It was clear to me that this would be a first visit, so I gathered all I could in the moment. I understood that the KHP would serve as an invaluable resource for the work The Horses were asking me to do.

More and more I was coming to understand that horses have a deep wisdom and ancient lineage. There is a change that is happening and we are being asked to live our lives in a more conscious, aware way. As we find ourselves in this time of great change and transition, the horses have important messages to share.

What I have come to understand is that Horses are here to assist not only in our healing, but also in our growth toward expanded connection and Higher Conscious Awareness. In my time with them, it has become very clear they are here on this Earth for a specific mission. I see this in their healing interactions with people who come to work with them and I hear this from the words and messages they share with me.

This book is a compilation of the horses' words to me and what they wish to convey to humanity at this time. Some of the messages come from the Horse Consciousness, which is the sum collection of all horse experience and knowledge, while other messages come from individual horses. The words are not my interpretation, nor my thoughts, simply what The Horses wish to be known by all. I am their vessel who gathers their wisdom and shares it with you. Thank you for reading.

THE COLLECTIVE HORSE CONSCIOUS

"It was long ago when we came.
We came to remind you of who you are.
We are part of you and we hold the key to you remembering all of Who You Are.
You are Love. You are Freedom. You are Joy.
You are expansiveness beyond limitation.
We as Horse, embody all of these characteristics
and yet you possess them as well.
And yet you seem to forget.
We have been here all along to remind you of your True Way.
Your True Nature.
In our interactions with you,
we show and share with you this True Essence of Being.
There are no limitations. There is no end to it. It just IS.
We carry these qualities throughout our entire being.
When you sit with us, you are connected to this essence.
But at times, you still seem to forget that we are simply showing you,
reminding you, of what you already possess.
There is no cost for it.
It is simply who you are.
And so we, collectively Horse, wish to remind you
of the expansive love that IS the human race.
Come back and remember this for yourselves.
Allow the memory and the knowing to course through your very being
*   and let it expand throughout the land and the world.*

Connect with us all and live in this state of bliss and knowledge. Be the Essence of Who You Are."

-The Horse Consciousness

HORSES AT WOLFTREE RANCH

Photo by Mindy Johnson

For the last five years, I have had the privilege and honor of living on nineteen beautiful acres in North Texas. It had always been a dream of mine to be able to live with and care for the horses in my life and create a healing space for people. This beautiful, magical land is set way back from the road in a very rural area and surrounded by woods on three sides with Lake Ray Roberts backing up to it. Many years ago I drew a picture of what I wanted our home to look like and I have to tell you that this ranch fits it almost to the last detail I drew out. I am the third owner of this ranch and the first to really live and create roots here.

The name of the ranch comes from the symbolic importance that wolves and trees personally mean to me. Wolf comes from the "imaginary dog" my parents told me I had around me when I was about three years old. When I took Sandra Ingerman's Introduction to Shamanic Journeying weekend workshop in 2003, I came to understand that this wolf was in fact my primary spirit guide, or Power Animal.

Trees have also held a sacred place in my heart throughout my life. I have always been drawn to trees. Even as a young child, climbing a tree and sitting there for hours was my safe place. I have always loved to sit with my back at the base of a tree and listen to all the ancient wisdom they have to share. When it came to naming this ranch, including these two important beings, trees and wolves, just seemed right. Like horses, I have a deep connection to trees and wolves. Each has helped me to unlock who I am and offered a way to connect with and honor this beautiful land where I now live.

The logical place to start is by introducing you to the seven horses who now live with me at WolfTree Ranch. When I initially began writing this compilation of wisdom in 2007, there were only three horses in my herd: Magno, Moonbeam, and Jingles. It feels only right to share their wisdom with you first. Since then, Spirit, Asante, Thera, and Domino have joined us adding to the magical nature of the equine facilitated program we offer through Horses, Heart & Soul ™, LLC.

Magno

"Courage is a most difficult essence to retrieve in a passage of Great Change.
All possess this gift even though some sense it to be elusive.
Walk with us and we will support you in drawing it out.
All courage is, is standing in your True Heart. Your True Essence.
Your Soul Path and connection to All at this time.
You humans possess so many gifts and talents.
It is easily in your path to open the doors and allow complete connection and
allowance of All that is you and wished for you by Spirit and your Soul.
Blessings on this path."

At the time of this writing, Magno is turning 17 years old. He has
been with me since he was 3 and half years old. To really get a feel
for him, you need to know that he is 17h, which would be almost six

feet at his shoulders. He is a Percheron/Andalusian cross gelding who is massive in physical size and incredibly gentle at heart. He came into my life a few years before Pooh died and my original intention in getting another horse was to help me with the transition of my beloved friend Pooh. I knew that the hole from Pooh's absence would be too much to bear and I wanted to have another horse in my life to continue the special kind of relationship I knew to be true with these beings.

You may laugh upon reading this but the reality check of how different Magno was from Pooh truly blew me away. I think at the time I was expecting to be able to connect with and partner with this horse in exactly the same manner as my relationship with Pooh. Well, I was absolutely wrong and I laugh at myself just reading and remembering the process that I went through with Magno. Magno wasn't Pooh. He had different lessons to teach me. He taught me, and continues to teach me, that in order to do anything in life, I have to be absolutely present, connected with myself, and committed to the process. When I am operating outside of this space, he will not play. I have had the joy of being reminded of this lesson in subtle and not so subtle messages from my beautiful partner. Sometimes it is a "look" from him that I have stepped outside of myself. Sometimes it has been an accident while we were riding or a jump refusal or even a stepped on foot.

This picture of the two of us is one of my favorites for several reasons. This was the first combined training show we competed in together. I was getting back into riding and we were learning how to jump together. The course we jumped on this day was only two feet – truly nothing for such a massive horse. What happened though during this course cemented several key pieces for me.

Halfway through our course, he went lame. I stopped him and saw that he was holding his foot funny. Where some might have pushed through or conversely quit, I jumped off him mid-course, picked up his hoof and saw there was a huge burr in his frog. My trainer threw me her keys and I pulled it out. He put his foot back down and looked at me saying," Come on! Let's finish this!" I am a vertically challenged person so mounting him is never easy, but all I needed was his encouragement to get my foot in the stirrup and move with his momentum back up in the saddle. You can imagine this is normally a challenging feat to accomplish. In this instance I was reminded of our incredibly strong connection. I moved light as a feather up and over and gently settled back in the saddle and we took off to our next obstacle.

Our next learning moment in this course had to do with a jump with a flower box at the base of the jump. Now, this is common occurrence to have a box of fake flowers at the base of the jump. It serves not only as decoration but also as a way for the horse to orient himself and calculate the spot from which to jump. Magno is afraid of these flower boxes so any jump we had previously worked with, he always had a moment of stopping and then jumping an extra two feet over it just to make sure his hooves did not come anywhere near the offending base. As we approached, I remember starting to worry about the flowers. Well since I stepped out of my confident space with him, he stopped. I heard him say, "Why should I do this if you aren't going to be in it with me?" He of course was right. So we turned and circled and I connected with my partner this time and looked straight at that obstacle. This was absolutely no big deal, I told myself. Together we can do anything. I stayed in my confident and present space and Magno jumped the heck out of that jump. Another picture I have of him he is clearing this obstacle by an three extra feet. WooHoo! When I look at this picture I see both of us smiling about not only for our accomplishment together, but also the lessons we just learned.

Magno's introductory words speak directly to who he is and his reminder to us. We all have inner courage to draw upon, yet we often forget how truly powerful we are. All we have to do is connect with our self and all will flow so easily from there.

Jingles

"Life is changing and shifting rapidly. All is the invitation that is being extended. Open your hearts. Past the pain and suffering that may exist. Do not let these things distract you. There is no belittlement of your experiences of pain, however, do not allow these experiences to keep you blocked and stuck within them. Allow these learnings to be acknowledged and move them on through to the earth where they can renew and recycle.. Once this awareness is in place, return to your heart and see that your soul is right there. The essence of all you are. This is the space Spirit wishes you to reside from."

I met Jingles at the barn where I boarded Pooh and Magno in Houston. At that time, the barn had taken over his care as his last owner stopped showing up and paying the bill. He turned into the barn mascot of sorts and helped build the confidence of many young horses. At this barn there were a number of racehorses and Mary Clark, the barn manager, began to turn Jingles out with the racehorses to keep them company. Racehorses tend to have a lot of energy. I'd watch a racehorse rip around the paddock and Jingles would just observe. Then after a bit Jingles would approach the horse and engage him or her in play. Jingles had a knack in helping the racehorses to connect and focus. He taught them how to move and release their excess energy. To see this Pony of the Americas with these large, gangly young horses so full of power and might always brought a smile to my face. He was a wonderful mentor and guide to each one of them.

Jingles had a history of being abused and neglected and the more I watched him, the more I saw how he had let go of his past and constantly took care of himself. At times, he would be off doing his own thing by himself in the pasture. When he wanted to play and interact with others (humans included), he would come back and join in the group. You always knew if Jingles had business with you because he'd walk right up to you and touch you or push you in the spot of your body where he was noticing something going on. After you made the connection, he'd walk away and go back to grazing. I like to call this his "Old Man Wisdom." He wants people to get the message he is sharing quickly and get on with the healing process. He does not like people remaining in a place of constant lamenting or holding on to old stories or beliefs about themselves.

He is the perfect reminder to us all that the past does not need to own us. It is certainly part of our life and our experiences and at the same time, we can connect to the lessons and the healing gifts from those events and continue to build ourselves into the beings we are invited to be in this lifetime. Jingles has his own way of healing. He spends time in his favorite pastures and I see him connecting with the earth and letting go of what he no longer needs.

Not only is he in tune with the earth and environment around him, he is also attuned to his herd and all that is happening with each one of them. He spends time with each member of his family on different days. I watch him impart his elder wisdom with each one of them always when it is clear they are working with something for themselves. When the conversation is complete, he walks on to allow his friends to integrate the new space they have stepped into.

Jingles' wisdom is to remind us, both horse and human, that our stories can but do not need to shape our lives and that the power to heal is within us.

Moonbeam

"I wish for all humans to see and acknowledge their own sacredness. Their own Being-ness. You are all such special loving creatures. We are here to remind you of your special gifts; to remind you of your purpose; to support you in clearing out the old so that you may rise into the High State of Being. This is a place of love, knowing and pure Soul connection. To remember the senses as gifts and guides on your path. We as beings love and treasure you as a group. It is why we came to be with you. Some of us show this to you as workers. Some of us as partners with you. Make no mistake, we feel, see and know all. We wish to remind you of these gifts in yourself. The gifts that are held within your heart that you may not always share with others. Those special essences that create You as YOU! We wish to assist you in re-connecting with them. It is through this connection that you return to the state of being one with your soul, your Spirit and the Spirit connection to All. Thank you for hearing this with your open hearts. Blessings on this Journey to you."

I have known Moonbeam for about eight years now. She is truly one of the most magical horses I have ever been around. I first met her at a children's residential home outside of Houston where I was given the opportunity to create a healing program between the children and the 11 horses living there. The first day I went to the program, I asked the Executive Director to take me to the barn to meet the horses. All 11 horses came running to the fence to greet us. Moonbeam looked me right in the eye and I heard her say, "There you are! We've been waiting for you."

Moonbeam is a natural as a caregiver. With both the herd and the children, she took on a Mother role. Even the kids who had the biggest walls built up around them could not keep their fortress in place when they were with her. After a few minutes of being in her presence, even if it involved simply standing in a stall with her, they would begin crying and release all the pent up emotions they had been holding in for so long. She would just look at them, move a little closer and hold space with them until they released everything they needed to let go.

Moonbeam came to live with Magno and Jingles in 2006. When we found our special ranch several years after that, she became the lead horse in their family herd. Her leadership style is one of cooperation and compassionate acceptance of all beings who come into her space, including the horses in her herd. She keeps everyone together and watches constantly to make sure of any changes in the environment to ensure the safety of all. Each time she works with someone they remark on her quiet strength and confidence and how she holds the space for each to remember these aspects of themselves. One person who worked with her called her "a brick wrapped in velvet." This is one of the most perfect descriptions of this mare I have ever heard. She is both solid and clear in who she is and what she asks of everyone and yet she communicates this in the softest of manners.

When I hear her words in her introduction, I see the reason behind why she will stand with a person as long as it takes. She waits patiently as they release all the spinning mind chatter and all of the agendas and the "have to's." She waits through the crescendo of frustration and into the peaceful state of acceptance, all the while standing quietly still. Once the person comes to this realization, she will wait another moment and then move with them. Moonbeam is a quiet beacon of strength in the storm of our human mental selves. She reminds us of the stillness inside and from that knowing, she facilitates the reconnection to our wonderful internal being that we are so often fearful of sharing with the outside. Moonbeam asks us to remember the inner wisdom of our heart and soul.

Spirit

"This space is a healing space, not like any other. I feel the ground/Earth vibrating under me like never before. It causes movement and shifting all throughout my being. My brothers and sisters in this herd show me the connection to all beings – animals, physical and mineral. I am the newest to this tribe and I see the connection to the humans on this land. We wish to help all beings open to their innate conscious awareness and lift all and everyone to the Higher Vibration that invites at this time.

I feel and see the movement of energy inside me. It is a wonderful glowing ball in my heart which connects to the core and expands and expands until it moves outside of me and invites all those around me to connect and expand. It is this purest form of love and heart which is the essence of soul. This is what I wish to share at this time."

Later in the year, Spirit wished to share about the concept of Physical Transition:

"This piece I know well as it is my lesson in this life. I am asked to bring in a whole new consciousness to my body. My body has been stuck in a stagnant place. I see the space of Flow all around. I see my body in the release. And yet my work is to let go of the old. It is very hard. My physical self likes this known way. It is rooted in this way. To make the shift I must lift myself from this original mold. I see this mold was created by others for me. I stayed in it as I did not know otherwise. Now I see with clear vision of the conscious way. I work with the release, which is based in fear, to clear myself and create my body as the free flowing view I see. I am almost there. When I remember to stay connected to all the love and support around me, I shift into my free, flowing being. It is a beautiful space. Hear my healing. Take a share in it for yourself."

Spirit joined our family about three years ago. He is a tiny Shetland pony who came to be with us when his original human family was no longer able to care for him. When he came to our ranch, I watched him look around and say, "What is this place?! What is going on here?"

The physical transition he speaks of is primarily around his hooves. When he came to be with us all four of his hooves looked like elf shoes – toes all pointed upward and all his weight back on his heels. Our farriers, Brandon Jones and Matt Horrall, and Christine Agro (clairvoyant and naturopath) have worked with him on a frequent basis to help his hooves return to a balanced state. Through this transition he has, at times, experienced pain and discouragement. I have watched him go through periods of wanting to give up and choose death, only to bounce back to a place of acceptance and perseverance in his healing ability. The other horses, Jingles especially, constantly remind him that he truly does have to ability to shift from this old space, this outdated picture of himself, to the high energy being he truly is.

One day a client noticed Spirit lying down out in the pasture. She became very worried about him and connected with his pain. I explained that he was hurting, and he had chosen to lie down and rest and to take care of himself. She wanted to stay with him so she sat down and meditated and he shared these words of wisdom, 'I see Joy in everything and so should you."

These days it is rare for Spirit to have a challenging day. He is the Joy and spark of excitement in this herd and welcomes every person who joins him with enthusiasm and a playful muzzle bump. As Spirit heals himself, he reminds us of our ability to do our own work by releasing the old and stepping into the new.

Asante

Photo by Teri Relyea Berbel

"The flow of the land that connects us is the energizing piece I share. I have been awakened to it once again after not knowing if for a long time. This way can come and go for those of us who are kept up off the land. For those of us who live most of our lives in a box.

As I step back into it the flow of the land, my body and soul become alive once again. It is a swirling motion that comes up into me from Mother Earth, through my feet. I remember again why I am here. At times I must have time/space to myself to re-body it. To remember it. It swirls up into me and expands throughout. This is not just a physical sensation. It is what you call a spiritual moment. Awakening is a beautiful way to describe this experience. This is why I am here. Why we are here. To share this awakening with you all. This is the energy of Spirit – of All That Is. It is why you feel calm and peace when you are with us. It is the way of energy about horses. It maintains All in balance and keeps The Flow. Remember this and allow this for yourselves. This is what surrounds Love to everywhere and anywhere. This is the energy of peace. As your book (the Bible) speaks of it – it is Peace that Passeth all Understanding. Go in Love and Peace."

Asante has been with us for over 2 years now. She is a beautiful 16h black Selle Français mare. In her previous life she was a show jumper and her owner shared her with us as she had hurt one of her legs, which resulted in the end of her show career.

Asante is shy at times and for the last two years has been working with her concepts of self worth and value in her new home. She has much energy buzzing around her at all times. I watch her work with learning how to channel this aspect of herself and create the balanced space she needs. Some days it is too much for her and she will take space away from the herd, or the herd will ask her to take some space. Other days she has that sweet spot of balance and being and flow that the horses talk about in this book. As I hear her words I see those "Awakening" moments she refers to and how she is completely infused by this energetic exchange. I look at myself and remember what this experience feels like and how "out of body" it can be – so much energy and vibrance at one time when one is not used to it can be overwhelming. Asante reminds us of the power of this experience- waking up- and that it is ok to take time to integrate it.

Thera

Thera is a mustang who was a member of the Pryor Mountain Mustang Herd. She shares her experience and insight of being a free horse among a herd who have been around humans all of their lives.

"Going from free to captive is a tortuous thing. My spirit exists still on my land. I long for it. I see it. I feel it. I do not always understand your ways. Why do you do the things you do with horse?

I see the loving bond that can exist. I feel it. I want to know it. And yet it is foreign and therefore I constantly look to see the value of trust in it. If I step into it, what will become of my free Flowing Nature? Does that change? Does it get taken away? Is that what you are wishing for from us (Mustangs)? This is the constant quandary for the free horse – or Mustang as you say. The old peoples understood this about us and there existed that free flowing energy between us (horse and human).

The walk of my kind when they come to people is how to balance the free nature of our being with your structured ways. It is very foreign to us. Keep this in mind when we come to your home. It is the important transition point – allowing freedom, Free Spirit, to flow in the nature of the confined way."

Thera joined our herd about two years ago, soon after Asante arrived. As I understand her history, she lived the first eight years of her life free with her family in Wyoming and the next eight years at a horse rescue who saved her from the slaughter house. She has remained an untouched horse. In the time she has lived here with us, I have followed my heart on the way that feels right to connect with her. It is not the way most trainers or horse professionals might go about it, but it is the way that feels right with her. I have invited her to say when she is ready to try new experiences, especially with humans, and therefore to have a say as to when she feels confident in connecting with the human perspective.

At this point, she and I can comfortably stand within an inch of each other – all the way around her body. She feels very comfortable touching me and will at times touch clients who come to work with her. She continues not to want humans to touch her. She constantly questions "Why?" when I work with her on the human concept of physical connection. To her, she sees our relationship as working perfectly where it is. She understands everything that is said to her – whether verbalized out loud or spoken from the heart. She is willing to participate as long as her space is respected. In this manner she is an amazing teacher about each being's right to set comfortable boundaries as well as how to create relationship without having your hands all over each other.

The most powerful healing she constantly works with me on is being in my heart. When I am in my heart, I am free and flowing. I am not weighed down with all the mental garbage, committees in my head, or past experiences. Instead, I am right in the present flowing moment with her. Her energy is so completely different from the other horses. She is so attuned to every minute nuance that exists around her and far beyond as well. She reminds us of the power of our sense and our abilities to experience the nuances, to listen to our body and our intuition, and our own heart wisdom.

Domino

"Finally I am here. I have waited a long time to be in a place that accepts me for who I am. So much loss and heartache have been mine. I have lost so many around me. So many have been unkind. This place is a Spiritual Awakening and finally my soul is at rest. I have come to teach the Way of Peace. Moonbeam speaks of this later. Peace is the only way. My body has been the vessel of so much "un-peace" in so many methods and at so many hands. Through it all I held the vision that Peace would come. I held my belief in this. I knew it would be. I wish for you all to know that even during times of pain, mistrust, misfortune – peace will come. This Earth is Peace. WE, Horses, are peace. Please hear our message and spread this through all of you. No more hurt is needed. Peace is the way to the heart and the true Essence that IS!"

Domino is the newest member of our herd. She is a seven year old Percheron/Paint cross. She arrived in the summer of 2013. What is interesting is that I met Domino two years ago at the horse rescue where Thera was living. She was in the stall next to Thera. Each time

I went to visit Thera, I would always stop and say hello to Domino. There was something about her that just drew me to her. She was very shy at this time but always said hello and accepted a carrot treat. At that time she had been adopted and was waiting to go to her "forever" home. Domino was born on a farm in Canada where pregnant mares were used for their urine to make the drug Premarin. When this farm was closed, all of these horses had to be rescued or else they would most likely end up at a slaughter house. Domino was under a year old when this occurred. She was saved by a horse rescue program in North Texas and lived with them until the time I met her in 2011. When she was adopted, she was unknowingly sent to a trainer who abused her very badly. She was returned to the rescue as Domino would not let anyone near her following this violence. When I found out she was available for adoption again, I immediately went to see her at her foster home. The foster parent had spent almost a year working with Domino to create trust with a human again. I visited Domino for about a month before bringing her home to WolfTree Ranch. Once she got here she settled in quickly and took over as the lead horse in the herd.

Domino's message of constantly looking for peace is seen everyday. She leads with a gentle firmness and it is very rare to see her use physical action against her herd members unless it is an absolute last resort. She continues to work on creating trust with all humans who come into her space each day. She has made tremendous progress in a short time and it is through her supporting other's healing that she experiences mutual healing with her self. Those who come to work with her always comment on the peace they experience in her presence and the way she brings them back into themselves and the present   moment.

INITIAL TEACHINGS

This first section is a compilation of writings I recorded following the shamanic journey I experienced in 2006. As I felt called by the horses to sit down and write, these are the pieces they wanted to share. These were collected over two years, at different times of the year. I typically would feel a pull to go and sit with my horses and always took my journal with me when I felt this calling. Some of these words come from specific horses and some come from The Horses as a collective entity.

I realize that some of this wording may feel "heavy" at times. And for me, it speaks to ancient wisdom being shared by horses and their collective spirit and history.

Easter Sunday
Moonbeam

"I am speaking for the NEW Beginning. The Day of today marks the new beginning of time, healing, rebirth and new growth. This day is a powerful energetic reminder of the Beginning of all. The Birds know it, the trees, the land, [and] the gardens. All beings know this. So for humans this day is for beginnings. To sit with the earth and connect. To feel the connection between both. She is the Mother. As the sitting connection is established, the root of the person connects to the earth - see this as a drilling down to the depths that feels correct. At that person's perfect depth, allow the unfolding of the cord. See the cord unfold, expand and spread far and wide. This spreading is the seeding of all intentions on this new day of the year. The person must intentionally state the idea for new growth, wish and it will then expand, spread to make the connections and grow to reality."

Balance

"We wish to speak of Balance on this day. Balance is the central core. It is the focus of all. Without Balance there is nothing. No matter the number of legs one possesses, all beings have a state of Balance that is innate and unique to each.

Humans forget this powerful core of themselves. Those who originally walked this land understood this harmony. Harmony is fluid connection to all. This connection extends not only to the relationships between all beings but the Flow that exists between animals, minerals, earth, trees, air, water, fire, wind, rocks and beyond. There are "particles" (you do not have the word for this feature yet available) that flow between all of us. That is how we sense the Essence. The Essence is what is carried through all beings. It is not measurable in a way you understand. It just is. It flows through every being and shares information as it is passed along. It is the essence that drives the flow of knowing and of passing time. This is an advanced concept. As the sun becomes presence, its rays exude the Essence and it begins the cognizant waking period of the day. There are many cycles for each being throughout the passing of the sun and moon. You will notice that some seem more "alive" or "awake" with the lights or with the darkness. All must honor their "natural" cycle and flow with that timing as it is significant to their purpose on this planet and during the particular life stage they are inhabiting. More will be spoken of the Life Stage later. In harmonizing or allowing this flow, the being is in balance.

This way has been abandoned by most humans. There is much talk by some of The Allowing and this comes from their sense and knowing of the Original Way, which is the way of the Original Intention that was created by Spirit. Spirit being the collective guidance that is the Keeper of All. The Originator of All is also a different subject for later.

So Balance exists when beings allow The Essence to flow in Harmony. This way of Being keeps the bodies of the spiritual, emotional, physical and cognitive selves in harmony and therefore in balance. The more beings step away from this innate process of Being, the more they experience of ill health - or disease as you named it. Each has their own cycle and the combination of all cycles creates unitarian balance for all. There is now great disruption as a significant number of beings (not just humans) do not allow the natural flow of Essence. We see this in land, trees, plants, minerals, air, water, fire, earth, animals and people presenting illness instead of healthness.

So our way is as we taught you before with the emotional flow. That flow is true for all the being states: emotional, physical, spiritual and mental. To allow the flow of consciousness of all as it is simply information allowing the flow of the Essence. Explore the ancient historical roots of this. As far as culture is documented, those original cultures practiced this way in all aspects of their existence."

Illness

"All beings therefore, have the ability to communicate with each other as this is part of flow harmony principle. Allowing the senses (all of them) to practice opening and listening and allowing the flow of information to pass through. The passing through is essential as we are all channels and the passing through keeps the essence going. When beings do not allow or hold for themselves or keep the essence inside, sickness prevails. We say it in this way as the essence is loaded with many levels and it forms structures of information. These stratospheres are not yet explained to you. Given the level of complexity it can be understood why holding of the information results in disease.

Those who hold it longer see drastic changes in their physical form. An example of this drastic form would be what you call cancer. We see this phenomenon as the ultimate example of not releasing and allowing. Where the information was mostly of a spiritual and energetic level, it is held for so long that the basic elements of each being take it on, envelope it and the essential messages then manifest and become part of the body.

The body does not have the specialty in mechanics nor the innate understanding to hold this high level of information. The body then tries to understand or "compute" within the body's systems. This works for a while and yet stops. It can no longer handle the unknown level of specialty processing of the Essence. The Essence is so embedded in the structure that it takes over. The body is not equipped for this takeover and then you see the phenomenon you call cancer. Cancer is the visual presentation of the high level Essence manifested in the physical form of the body. Your creation of medicine may help for a time but usually, at this point, it is too late - but not always. The Essence is still movable but it takes great commitment on the will of the individual who is experiencing this state."

Empaths

"Empaths are of this world and not. This is a Divine gift that they possess. It is given to those who speak from their heart at all times. The issue at this time with the current Empaths is that their hearts are closed. The horses wish to especially work with humans in the process of opening their hearts. As this is their desire, their goal, and the way they wish to bring this work. It is through the heart, it is the connection of the soul and also the name of your business which is why they choose you to help this healing work with the humans through their (The Horses') way.

Empath is a word that does not accurately describe the ability that a human has to do this work. This gift comes from a space far far away. We do not mean this to sound as an intergalactic space fantasy however. It is a gift that has come from another place. It did not exist before previously to this planet. As horses work with their body, and all is through their body, or their tool, and this ability comes from beyond this planet Earth. An Empath who is in balance is able to work completely through their heart. They take in information through their heart, it spreads all throughout their body and beyond, and will be able to read anything and everything that comes into their presence. This is the same as the horses do.

With humans at this time, it is incredibly difficult for them to access this ability as there is much pain and hurt and anger and fear that overtakes the heart. As you see there are more and more who must go to your doctors, searching for a cure for their heart related ailments. This is because people are not using their body in the way it was gifted to them originally and therefore there are many blockages, most especially in the heart. An Empath is able to see with their heart, feel with their heart, know with their heart, understand with their hearts, and hear with their heart. They know how to open that Grate of which we speak and then when to close, once enough information is passed through. They hold nothing and they release everything.

Another issue that humans need to be aware of is returning themselves to balance. It is the Empath's job and their calling in this lifetime to share their gifts and help others return to healing and balance. That is nature of the Empath. That was the original intention of the Empath.

However at this time, you will notice that those people who are truly Empaths are incredibly overwhelmed by all the information that comes at them. This is because the information is coming from the Flow. The Flow does not judge and therefore the Flow sees the individual as the Empath they are. The Flow will notice this person as a conduit to hear the information and assist in the healing for the individual or others around them, for the region, planet and world in entirety.

The Empath in this world is not equipped to deal with this ability as it is not taught to them. These ways are no longer taught as that ended with the Original People, who were removed from their land and not allowed to continue practicing their way as Nature intended. So it is with you Divine One, that we ask, show you, and teach you the way of working with the Empath. You are one as well and learning to balance your field and continue the Flow of all through you. The Horses teach this well.

The person who is an Empath must allow all information to enter through their hearts, flow throughout their being where they gather the information needed, and then allow it to pass on through. Each Empath has her/his particular way that they allow the Flow to occur and where the flow goes. By that we mean the Flow exists through each Empath, as their own unique I.D., their own trademark stamp on it, if you will. Envision a body and the information, or energy, flowing to the body, through the body, and out the body. This release is passed on to the next Empath with an extra action where it will be carried by the Helper to the next destination point, or where it is next needed.

Empaths in this world today are in great need of assistance and learning how to work at their gifts. Most especially the children who are being born into this world at this time. The majority of them are considered to be Empaths and yet they are being medicated at this time and not well understood. More of this work will come. More of the Healers will come to work with these children. Different Healers are called to work with the children at each of their life stages to assist them in their growth and learning as a developing Empath."

Guardians

"Each entity on this planet, and everywhere for that matter, has a guardian. No matter whether it has two legs, four legs, slithers across the earth, crawls on its belly, or swims in the ocean or the sea, all creatures have guardians. These guardians come from great distances beyond and from the Great Light that comes from The Creator or Spirit. Each entity, or presence, as it is born into this life on this earth or on this plane is gifted with a guardian.

The Guardian is different than the shamanic version of the power animal. The Guardian comes into this world with the person (as we are mostly speaking about humans as those who read this book are mostly human). Guardians are part of the human and yet not. They come from the energetic space of the human that the human is unaware of. They are all that the human is, and all that the human is not aware of yet at this time or know about him or herself. This being gently guides and interacts with the person at all times.

*Even though the person may not be aware, they feel like they have a "guardian angel" following them. They feel incredibly lucky or as if they just knew something was about to happen. Or maybe it felt like somebody whispered in their ear. This is their Guardian who is walking with them. When the person feels that there is someone right behind them or right around them. When they are in deepest, darkest despair, anguish or pain and then they feel comforted and lifted up. That is their guardian who is working with them at that time. Each person can know their Guardian. All they have to do is sit, get quiet, and ask. The Guardian will reveal itself but only when asked. Part of the Guardian's learning in this role is to prepare to be incarnated after their charge leaves this world. In a way, this is training for the Guardian before it comes to this **Flow of Life**.*

There are many different beliefs on this subject of Guardians and incarnating after their human charge transitions. This is the view that we wish to share at this time. You may ask your guardian to walk with you for a variety of themes. You may ask for courage. You may wish for answers to questions or help finding clarity or even assistance in releasing and healing. The Guardian is always fair and simply wishes to be asked to be of service. That is the role of the Guardian. Guardians exist to give love and be of connection."

The Grate

"The Grate is not as you think. It is simply the golden protective mash that sits over this Holy Place on the physical body. It was given by God/Spirit as the being manifested in the physical realm. It is their signature I.D., if you will, that is with them as they take in, allowing pass on The Flow. You have the power to open your Grate and allow Flow in, through, and onward.

A Grate is the door to the heart which ultimately is the opening to the soul. All beings possess a Grate. Each person's Grate, each being's Grate is perfectly created, especially for their unique individuality. Some are small, some are large, some are constructed of a variety of material.

The purpose of the Grate is to allow a protective covering over the heart which is the essence of, the True Essence of, the individual. When people have been hurt, not been able to protect themselves, or not paid attention to, understood, or even known of The Flow and how it pertains to their self, their life, and their world, their Grate may be damaged. And therefore with this damaged or compromised Grate, the person or being, is unable to safeguard their body, if you will, from the Flow or over Flow of information. This Grate exists for even and balanced flow of all information, in and throughout, moving on out the body and beyond.

A compromised Grate may be restored, renewed or rejuvenated simply by saying and setting the intention of healing for the Self. Through this intention setting, the Grate will naturally be restored and the body will return to its national state of balance. It IS this easy to return to healing, to return the body to balance and allow the Flow to continue on through.

Many individuals believe that it is incredibly difficult and impossible, to use a human word, to restore one's own body, one's own Self, to healing and balance. This is untrue and we wish to stress how easy it is for each individual- no matter where they come from, no matter how many legs they possess, if they are planted in the earth or what their status on this planet is. Each individual, each Being has the ability to restore its Self to balance and health and wholeness.

It is very important, especially at this time in this world, that all beings understand and remind themselves and know and practice the return to balance. This planet is about to go through incredible shift and change and it is very important that all be in balance to prepare and assist this world and Others in this transitionary period."

The Rain

Moonbeam, Magno and Jingles

"We wish to tell you of the rain. We feel the vibration shift in the air. Some of us experience the shift so vibrantly that we react with our bodies which is why you see us jumping and running when the storm is coming. Some of us sense it before your professionals do. Those of us with that ability pass it on through the region so that all can prepare and get right for the weather change. **In that we mean ready our bodies and channels so that this shift can flow on through and any and all information is passed on.**

You will notice as we position our bodies, we move with the wind so that the wind and energy, or information, goes all the way through from back to front. This is different from the way we typically welcome in the Flow (front to back). This difference is also about clearing and cleansing.

The wind and loud, clear storms sift through our channels. Sifting and cleansing and resetting anything that is in need of adjustment. You noticed today that we also shifted and moved toward each direction. Not only were we honoring each of the directions, but also connecting with the medicine of the North, South, East and West.

The storm comes in from the direction that needs the healing spread on the land and all living there first. This restores the harmony and balance (as much as possible) with that initial **Directing Direction.** *It then shifts either counterclockwise or clockwise as needed. We move with these shifts not only to clear ourselves but also as* **Assistant to the Director.** *One of our many roles is restoring balance. As the one who wrote Animal Speak, [Ted Andrews] wrote of us symbolically that we walk between both worlds. Because we are of this way, we are responsible for shifting and focusing and restoring balance on the land. Some of us do this for our own* **"property"** *we are physically situated on. Some work with the region. Some are called to work with even larger areas, quadrants, countries, planets and universes.*

Spirit guides and directs the storms or cleansing where it is needed and all is in Divine timing. We'll **speak more of draught and other conditions.** *We are more of* **the Lakota way** *with the Directions and meanings. They* *understand us as teachers and healers and Medicine Beings. They of all **The People** are most connected to us. Yes, there is variance in the traditions, symbols and representations among us, as is common with The People and those who study The Light Way as well. Research more the Lakota connection with Horse Medicine and we will guide you."*

The Integration of the Herd

Moonbeam

*"We **incorporate** each other. That is to say, each of our energies or fields or sense of awareness, individually greets the others. The fields reach out to each other and sense or feel each other - there is actually not a human term for this event. But basically it is the field reaching out with fingers, with a level of unimaginable sensitivity.*

The fingers touch, meet and greet. Each has their own "synthesis code" or I.D. Markers. There are a variety of ID markers on each field. They tell and mark each of us. So in this exploration of each other's field markers we learn the stories of each of us - in this life and all our other lives. So we immediately have the knowing and understanding through this download of any and all information. Plus we also learn of the assignments we are each given in this lifetime. This is tremendously important in joining herds as we must each understand our role and destiny, if you will, in this current physical realm.

This water spot (tank on the land) is important for all of us as it balances all of these things. We meet over the water and she extends her liquid and flowing healing throughout all the fields and into each of the markers. She is soothing all.

You as humans view our coming together and joining from your own perspective. What is truly happening is we are experiencing and taking in so much information at one time, that it can be overstimulating and therefore you see our bodies on high alert. Moonbeam shows how she interacts with [a new horse] nosedown on the ground with his. She allows him to experience her markers and then she attempts to share her wisdom with him. It is too much and he moves away. She waits in a neutral place until he assimilates a bit more. Magno then comes - he is young and drawn to the interaction. Again it is too much at once so each boy moves a bit to allow flow and all the way through - nothing is stuck. The Wise Ones, Moonbeam and Jingles, keep the younger ones moving in order to remind them of the Way of Flow and always keeping the body being in balance.

These four have accepted each other and their field of wisdom. Each has a role to play in terms of teaching, sharing, experiencing and guiding. They have achieved the neutral space of acceptance."

Sitting Bull speaks of Acceptance:

"All is and will be in this earthly life plan. It is not to be judged or ignored. It is for experience and love. For with this way comes peace that passeth all understanding. This is the Way of the Flow these special beings teach. They were brought to this earth to teach this way. It was known and practiced before and now has been set aside. It is why they wish you to write their way."

Grace, Flow and
The Way of the Horse

"This is the path we wish for you to be our speaker. You see and feel and experience our way. You see beyond what is. This is the path of Flow and The Way of the Horse. The layers of subtlety, that is Grace. Grace expands through all and throughout. It is a main messenger in each of these markers. As the others [other humans knowledgable of horses] speak of us as always looking to be in relationship, it is truly about the expansion of Grace. Grace is the meditator of Flow. She is the Ambassador. The Welcomer. The Guide. The Intuit.

She opens the way for the Way of Flow as she is The Way. With Grace, all is open and balanced and even. There are no rough edges, as Grace allows all to come as they are. There is no "right" or "wrong" way. It just is. It is the I Am that presents in your meditation. Grace is. You are. I am. He is. She is. We are. Grace is. Flow exists. Flow expands. All is brought in balance."

Transitions

"Humans have much fear of transition. They have forgotten the way of living with and in harmony with the land and All around them. There are rituals to be honored and practiced before all shifting. Since that is all a transition is: a shift.

This shift can be physical, emotional, or spiritual. Mental can cause distraction of the need/request/desire of shift. The desire or request of the shift may not come from the individual. It may come from the Guide, Guardian, Helping Spirit, Teacher or even Spirit as a complete whole.

Humans have forgotten they are not in charge, but believe themselves to be in control. With this way of practice comes a difficult and challenging journey as they are not co-creating or aligned with Spirit. When we are aligned and working with Spirit, all flows smoothly. We take in, experience, understand and then release and pass on the information around us. We allow the Flow to guide us. This is the Way of the Horse. It is actually the Way of All Beings who are connected with the Flow.

At this time on this planetary plane, all beings are asked to return to this conscious alignment of being. This Way of Being will facilitate the transition coming very soon to this earthly plane. This is one of the main purposes of Horse at this time. Of course another main purpose is returning to balance and knowing of Self and all that is around. It is why we wish this book written. Our way is very important for humans at this time period to understand.

Our transition at this time (moving to our new home) involves physical relocation. With this knowing, we are able to take in all information from The Flow. The Flow passes through us to teach of what is to come. Not only do we prepare ourselves for this change in space, but we also prepare the land we currently are connected with, the path of the transition space, and the land we are moving toward. There is much ritual involved in transition. Each herd has a member who is designated to prepare these Ritual Paths."

The Ritual

"This is a most sacred and honored tradition. Another piece that we bring back to humans at this time as they have stepped away from all of their indigenous learning and ways. This is not a criticism, simply an observation. Before, we were part of all Ritual. We taught ritual to you.

Before any change occurs in our gathering, we prepare ourselves. We sense the coming of change and some of us are more sensitive to this than others. It comes to us as we have taught you, in a wave of the Flow of energy. We experience it with all of senses and our entire being at once.

As some of us are more sensitive, it may be too much at one time which is why you witness those of us with this way of experiencing to be "high strung" or constantly running or being nervous or jumpy. It is because of the energy that is flooding our bodies and it is much to process and move through so some of us must move to assist it in transitioning through.

This is very similar to some humans who have been referred to as "too sensitive" or "reactive" or "too emotional." They are experiencing the same issue, but have no one to teach them what is happening and how to process it. For us, we move with it. As we move with it, we understand the information and allow it to flow through and pass it on to others. It never stays because if it were to stay, it would create complete disharmony in our bodies. So we ask that when you see us in this state, to give us space so that we can process what is happening in that moment. It will move through and we will return to our individual natural state of being.

As we prepare by taking in and experiencing the information as it is presented, there is one of us who keeps the information, one who passes it on, one who guards the others while the flow is transmitted, and one who holds the Sacred Space of Being. If we are a smaller group, not all the roles may be needed. If we are one in the herd, other helpers from nature will assist us. Sometimes humans are even part of this process. For you, be aware of how you feel when you are with us during states and times of transition. You will quickly discover if we have incorporated you in a role within the herd.

Some of us have a challenging time with transition...just as some humans do. We like where we are, our routine, our way, our humans, our surroundings. Sometimes we don't want change to occur, even though we know part of our being at this time is to be a Teacher of Peaceful Transition through ease and grace. So like humans, we understand this experience. Which is why some of us are so bonded to our humans who also experience this challenge in life.

When we do experience this challenge, we find ourselves surrounded by our ancestors and they sit with us while we experience the challenge until we have moved through it and it is released. There is no "right" or "wrong" way of Being. Each way is perfect for the individual, no matter how many feet they have or their existence in this plane. That is an important piece of this teaching. Each Way is perfect.

So in making the transition…no matter what it is…we prepare the space we have been in. By space, this can mean a thought, an actual place, a learning, an experience, one we interact with…there are a myriad of meanings to "space." We honor it first by acknowledging the presence it has held in our life. We honor it for the learnings we have received from it and from the healing that has occurred from it being in our life at this time. We thank it for all it has shared and taught and done. Usually "the space" will return the sentiments. We do this collectively and individually as there is always an individual role in addition to the role it played with the herd.

Once gratitude has been expressed, we ask for release from connection of the space. We can always revisit if needed or asked (on a spiritual or actual physical basis), but it is important to release the ties to the old space so that we can move forward into the new space clean and clear and without attachments. It is holding on to those old attachments that invite blocks of energy which in turn result in disharmony in the state of being.

This can also lead to sickness (emotionally, physically, mentally or spiritually) and sometimes death. We say death because there are times that a being is so connected to the old space that they are no longer able to function in the new. Their body shuts down as it refuses to assimilate the new information. When this occurs, the other members of the herd, as well as helping spirits, attempt to work with the individual, but it is truly up to the individual to release and move into the new space or stay committed to the previous space.

Before we move to the new space, the energy from us is sent ahead. Like we described before, this flow is passed on by all in its path and goes to the space to prepare. In this scouting kind of preparation, the request is made to come into the space in a respectful manner and answered at the same time so that we know we are being welcomed and we have asked permission to join and connect in a respectful manner.

Once we receive this reception, we begin to send our energetic self to the space, so that the space gets to know us and our energies can all combine together and create a new Flow that is ready for all that is coming. The space is therefore prepared before we arrive so that when we get there, and you see us alert and checking everything out. We are looking for all parts of ourselves and the combination of all the new energies. Again, this is an experience of new energies that we are experiencing and assimilating and therefore why you view us in a heightened state of alertness and activity.

Once the energy of our actual physical presence has joined the current energies of the new space, we are able to relax into the new space of Being. We spread our energy out and experience the new connection(s) to our self and all that is around us. The herd will be different as we have blended with the new space and that shifts all in us as well. It is important at this time to give us space and time to adjust. Some of us will take a day. Some will take more. Like humans, each is different and has their unique way of adjusting and integrating. Once the Flow is balanced, the space and all in it, return to the neutral place of balance and ease."

Taken Over By Fear Versus Standing in and Trusting in Love

"This is the most important of all for us to share. Love is what the universe and Spirit are made of – fear is a human construct.
All of the energy gets wrapped into this dark, powerful expression that takes over and manifests the deeper seed of disconnect."

THE KENTUCKY HORSE PARK

As it was my experience at The Kentucky Horse Park that continued to energize my creativity, it is from this place that I carry on the story. The first set of writings in this section took place during my initial visit to the park for the Rolex Three Day Event Competition in 2006. During breaks of watching the horse/rider partners compete, I went to visit the History of the Horse Museum and also sat at Man O' War's grave for the first time.

Man O' War was one of the greatest Thoroughbred racehorses of all time. Even walking toward his magnificent statue makes one want to genuflect in reverence to acknowledge the awesome power and presence that continues to envelope his memory. As I sat by his grave I heard his words flow.

Words from Man O' War

Man O' War spoke of the essence of horses in competition and the Spirit of their energy and hearts in the arena of performance:

"I am the speaker for all of us. I speak for all when I say how much gratitude, peace and reverence we have for you. In this visit, in the listening and in the writing of our way, you who are small in size, are mighty in power. I will explain to you of the power I speak of. This is what you felt as the horses came towards you in the event [the cross country trial]. You notice that some had great expanses and some did not. You noticed many varying degrees and this is all true.

What you felt is a combination of God/Spirit and their soul which is housed together in their hearts. This energy system (and it is system)... this system exists in all. Humans, for the most part, forget or turn off, if you will, this gift that exists in all. It is how we operate for lack of a better word. Those who will read this will understand "operate" better at first. As it is truly about Flow which connects all to everything.

So as you witnessed the Black Guardian horse on the hill after the accident [one of the competing horses fell at one of the cross country obstacles], *you saw that he was receiving the wind/She Who Shares the Information With her Breath. That is how the wind is... More will be shared on this by She herself as we know she works with you divine one. Yes that is what we call you and yes you are worthy of this. Like I said, you are small in size and mighty in power.*

*This Flow you observed the Hill Guardian (*a horse was standing on the hill by one of the cross country obstacles, clearly watching all that was happening with each of the horses throughout the course) *taking in was information from the event* being passed to him. *He also was taking in information as to the whereabouts of all the others and getting ready to share what happened to prepare and warn or caution the other athletes. All of these courageous athletes are connected. The Hawks you saw overhead were the Watch Guards of the sky and also sharing the Flow to the Guardian. His lip action was taking in and releasing almost like a telegraph. The two leggeds understand not the purpose of these noble guardians. The guardians set up the idea for them through The Flow to have them staggered throughout so they may relay information to all.*

*Some of the horses are well-suited to this competition job and some are not, as you saw in the pair that rode past (young girl and dissociated horse). The one called Teddy is however. You experienced his energy more than others because you know this from your **Guardian** Pooh.*

*We also wish you to know they walk with the same energy. Those who are Seers see you surrounded with a great Light. Those who are **Empaths** feel this in you and is why they comment on your energetic presence. Those with **Darkness** in and around them see and feel this energy in you and are drawn to it. But their drawing to is more wanting what is yours and not sharing and creating for **the Greater Good.** That which you felt from Teddy, you felt most strongly because you are on a similar path and similar energetic and vibrational level. It causes the heart to radiate a love which is the ultimate expression of your soul.*

*The next piece in the learning is to allow and invite that vibration to be when it is in **The Being State.** You will be shown how to **open the Grate** and allow the Flow. You already communicate in the Flow as you hear, share and pass on the information to all. It is why the horses looked directly at you this weekend and why the trees had you capture their physical presentation and the re-creation of their souls as pictures. You will sit with them as they have individual pieces to teach as well."*

Man O' War

Part II

This next set of writing occurred during my second visit to the Kentucky Horse Park in the summer of 2010. I spent many hours writing the words from the horses in the History of the Horse Museum as well as through The Gift of the Horse exhibit.

"Oh yes, I have been waiting for your return. You have been missed dear one. The time is now to record our sayings and bring our words to the human race. You are the one we wish to speak for us as you feel our hearts and souls. This is your gift…to feel the hearts and souls of others – all others – whether they be human, animal or mineral. All that you feel is your gift. Remember this.

I begin the history tour as most will know of me and I bear credence in this world. You visited with our relations today at [The Hall of Champions] and began to feel the vibration of our ancestry. It is old and very ancient and the wellspring of the original vibration of the earth. Most especially these Arabians who are the beginnings of us all.

You will note that their history and lineage is not all complete as most of the records are lost. But you will feel what needs to be said and that is what you will write.

*We, those offspring of the Ancient Ones carry their vibration inside of us. It is what gives us Life's Breath. Every muscle of our being, every fiber inside calls to us, the Ancient Ones. They run with us and surround us. This is part of what must be said and known. As your race has disconnected itself from this Knowing. This is part of what we wish you to bring back…the Ancient Knowing of all that is connected inside, from before and beyond. (*A leaf from the oak tree I was sitting under fluttered down and landed next to me as I was writing*) This oak leaf which chooses to sit with you is an example. In it you can see the striations of who it is today but also what it comes from. We are much the same. You are much the same. When I run, because I still do…only in Spirit Form* *now…I feel all the Ancestors within in me and around me. I now run with those who run in the present time. They feel me in their blood, their bones, in their hearts.*

When you experienced the heart of Teddy, beloved horse of Karen O'Connor, you felt this connection to all that was before him, but All that still is in him. This is the way we all feel. It will be challenging to put into words that visceral experience you had but you must…as it is important to share with those you will share this document with. That is what we all walk with. Stand with. Present ourselves with. It is the Heart and Soul of Horse. The Way of the Horse is to stand in complete and total connection with all we are and all who came before us. If your kind would open themselves to this state and way of being, you would feel this utter connection of completion and line that is Without End.

When we came to this place (Earth) it was part of our teaching to share with all around us. Some of the humans understood this – the Ancient Bedouin, the Mongols, the Native Americans – all of them felt and knew this completely, Heart and Soul. This is part of why you have your title (Horses, Heart & Soul ™, LLC) as you do. Because the inside of you knew what this means and felt the experience. Your precious Pooh reminded you of this knowing and Linda's book [The Tao of Equus] brought you back into this knowing fully.

The Old Ones felt this connection from their steed partners and understood that this was a teaching from them as well. This is why they are known by your kind as "great horse tribes" as they opened themselves, and for some, re-opened themselves to this deep knowing and space of being. Some of them came from other places to teach their tribe this way. Some were born into their tribe with this contract, and some realized this was their path in that lifetime. They lived Heart and Souls with the horses around them. They knew and felt and experienced all that their horses did and were able to expand themselves not only through the partnership with their horse, but also with knowing of the land, Spirit and All around them and beyond."

Secretariat

Secretariat, another great racehorse in the history of America, is also buried at the Kentucky Horse Park. In sitting at his grave, he had words to share as well.

"You feel me just in watching a human made movie. I am the visceral experience that Spirit wanted to share with a world that was very troubled and filled with Darkness in a bleak and limit filled time and way. Spirit showed and shared through me the way of expansion, the way of heart, the way of soul completely unfettered and open and expansive. To bring the humankind back to their essence and remember theirs hearts and ultimate calling on this land. This is the gift I shared with the peoples of my time. The woman understood this and without words, but through her actions, worked to share the essence or being in Spirit with all around. She felt it and knew it and conveyed it through her passion and purpose. She lived as Spirit."

The Ancient Horse

After sitting with Man O' War and recording his wisdom, I was guided to return to the KHP's History of the Horse Museum. The original ancestors of the horse wished to share a bit of their history for this project. It felt very important to document the earliest beginnings of this creature and why they originally showed up and the reasons behind their disappearance.

While I do reference some history of the original predecessors, the focus is not on the archeological facts. It is simply the words of these ancient beings around their intention, purpose and timing of their presence on the earth.

The Dawn Horse

The Dawn Horse is the original ancestor of the modern day horse. They showed up in North America around 55 million years ago and then migrated north across the Bering Strait and into Eurasia.

The Dawn Horse was the size of a fox and had a four fingered foot. The Dawn Horse transitioned to the Pleistocence Horse who existed until 10million years ago when it vanished. Scientists say they disappeared due to the Ice Age and the land no longer supporting them.

When I asked these Ancient Ones in the museum what happened they replied:

"We came so long ago…we still whisper the song of God. It blows amongst us. We came to share the way of Spirit…to be shared in our way, The Way of the Horse. We came to share the deep knowledge of the earth and the sky and all in between. It took many moons to share this…at the beginning time was not right. Your kind were still figuring themselves and their way. Gradually they came to watch us and how we were with the world. The earth. Connected to All. They saw this and began to follow suit. We are the Beginning Messengers of All Time. This concept you know…and will know more of. The humans of that time began to regard the earth as sacred and to move in relationship with it. Once this connection was made, the people did not struggle. All Flowed from All – within and throughout. This was our way in this time.

We left for awhile as the human changed and did not honor the earth for awhile. Fear presented in the Dark Times (cold period). We had to go and wait to return when warmth came back. At this time, the people were able to re-connect with their deep knowing of Flow with the Earth and all around."

As I continued through the museum exhibit, I saw that horses disappeared from North America, but were still found in Europe, Asia and Africa. Not only were they part of war, transportation, and the building of civilizations, they were, in some worlds, part of daily culture and family.

There are certainly many breeds and facets to the history of the horse. What is documented in this book is what I was directed to focus on by the horses themselves. In no way is it any omission of any horse or time period, nor a slight on their history or development. I am simply staying true to the voices of the horses who are telling the story.

The Mongolians

The Mongolians were known as nomadic horse people. Horses lived with them as part of their family. I found an old Mongolian saying that "A Mongol without a horse is like a bird without the wing."

Attila the Hun was descended from Mongolian tribes. Even though he is known as a barbarian and ruthless killer, he spoke as well:

"As much as those who tell my stories today wish to see me as an evil entity, I knew the Way of the Sacred One, what you call the horse. That pulsating heart that is pounded out through the four connectors to the earth and the vibration being passed along to all around and beyond. That is the Flow of Spirit come transcended to this earth and this plane. This pulse is the way Spirit moves...the ground experience is what moves the beings all around and spreads the "word" along. By this I mean the translations of all the energy being passed from one being to another. From one experience and on, so that all are informed and in effect, connected to The All, which is Spirit. I knew these things in my heart. As a warrior, I could not always share my lead with the Heart, but had to portray in a way that my people would understand. The horses with me in that land knew who I was and saw my heart. I felt and saw theirs and the connection and communion between us all. This is why we had great connection and compass across the lands at this time."

The Mongolian Horses Speak

"Ahhhh.....we are running, running, running. To stay afloat, adrift. To keep our ancestral heritage in tact. Those who come to visit us are drawn by our calling. We are the Old Ones. The Masters of the Battle. The Way of Hardy Living. We know The Code of Spirit. The Original Ways of Being with The Land and All around us. The peoples know this about The Way and know Us. We are the base of the original code that is now Horse today. Feel our stride. Hear our hoofbeat. It is the sound of Spirit. We run with The Wind. She carries us and like the Arabs said, We came from the Wind and She is part of our hearts and

souls. The Wind is part of our True Essence. The Wind carries our message, our being, our Spirit. The Wind is Spirit. We fly and fly and fly…far, far beyond- in this world that you see and The Other Beyond. The Other is that which you may not "see" but you know is there. That you feel is there. That your senses pick up and carry on and on and on. We are Messengers of Spirit. To remind you of your courage and bravery. That you are Spirit as well. That no matter where you are, you can call upon this Essence of your Self and BE Spirit! That is our message. Humans must be Spirit at this time. The old warrior ways of your current people is not the way. It has caused much pain and drama and damage to all and everything. Mother Earth is crying from all the death and destruction. Hear Her! Hear Us! Redeem this way and move to The Way of Spirit. The Way of Horse. The Time Is NOW!"

Bucephalus

Alexander the Great was a contemporary of Attila. They actually fought each other. There is a powerful story of how Alexander came to be with his horse. A great horse, named Bucephalus, was brought to King Phillip, Alexander's father. A magnificent gift for the king. However, no one was able to even get close to this horse as he bucked and reared and fought anyone who attempted to come close to him.

Alexander was 12 at the time and being groomed to be king. He told everyone he could mount this horse. The way the story is told, upon watching Bucephalus, Alexander realized the horse was afraid of his shadow so he spent time leading the horse toward the sun so he was unable to see his shadow. After several days of the doing this, the horse trusted him and allowed him to get on his back. From then on, the two were tied together. Many great stories were written on the relationship between Bucephalus and Alexander, in particular their war time relationship.

However in sitting with the image of Bucephalus, a different version was shared:

"I was seen by the great boy king...as I knew that only a child would still be able to see through his heart at this time on the earth. He saw my heart with his heart. He was not ever able to share this ability with others as they taught him the way of the human – which is to see through the head and mind. In honoring his gift of sight, I showed the world around him how to connect no matter the outer perception of power and prestige. But through the heart. This boy felt my heart from far away. I felt his from far away. The communion between us existed as such. It is what we possess and wish to re-share with humans at this time. The Way of the Horse is the The Way of the Heart is the Way of the Soul is The Way of Spirit is The Way of the Horse."

Fairy Tales and Myths

During the Dark Ages, the horses even tried to connect with humans and get their attention...

"We spoke to the people through myths...at that time they needed to believe that we were part of them. A symbol of their strength and personal power. It was through this way that we again taught of The Way of the Horse, although hidden in the Way of the Ego of humankind...our message still came across and the story was shared and passed along for many times."

If you think about it, any Heroine, Knight, or Hero who went out on a quest, did so with only a horse as a partner; the valiant, noble steed. The Hero's powers and qualities were always enhanced through the description of the horse. Myth and fairy tales wrote horses into the stories as the connection between conscious and unconscious. Horses were the link between "the quest" and the true, ultimate journey of personal and spiritual development.

There were several other humans showcased in the Museum of the Horse exhibit that were involved with horses. They had powerful thoughts to share as well.

Charlemagne

"Almost as a saint I was revered...the peoples felt, unknowingly to them, the essence of the Spirit through the horse in my presence – my being. I saw this way from the beginning with them and saw the balance of power, and the true Spirit of the Warrior of them. That love and seeing through the grounded way of the heart was the most powerful way. Once stepping into this way, the way of the horse, I felt the Flow unfurl like a brilliant flag flying through battle. The peoples around me responded to this way and fell in with The Flow of All. It was a beautiful sight to behold. Even in this stained glass window depiction (Charlemagne Window at the Cliché Museum in Paris) *I see the horse and I connected to Spirit and the knowing that expands between us and surpasses the "challenge" in front of us. A valuable lesson for us all, eh non?"*

Leonardo Da Vinci

"I saw the movement of the flow of energy in this majestical body of this Spiritual Beast. In these Dark Times, I could not speak of what I knew, what I felt, what I experienced as surely I would have been locked away and killed slowly. I knew that part of my experience, my calling as you say, was to document the movement of The Flow of the universe. The horse was a magnificent example of such, even though those around Him did not see this...for the most part. I saw the energy flow from between his ears, down his neck, rippling across his shoulders and shuddering through the back and haunches and then out the tail and onward. On to the next recipient of the information to be taken in and shared. It is how this Flow operates. In through the top of the body, all throughout and across and then passed on and on. It is the base of this body language way that humans try to describe what they see in these Spirit beings. They need no words. Their experience is All. They are pure love and energy. This is the Essence of Spirit. My meager works attempted to share what I saw and knew deep inside."

Horse Breeds

Part of the main exhibit in the museum was dedicated to honoring the many breeds of horses found today. While this section does not cover even a fraction of the number of breeds that exist, these were the horses who wished to share their wisdom for this book.

The Thoroughbred

"The Thoroughbred is the In Between of us all. They possess the magnificence of Spirit, the Grace of the Flow of All, and the power of the physical incantation of the Earth. Their flatout stride is total expansion of the Self and Being. It is the heart's expression of opening up to all of ones' infinite and complete possibilities of their contract in life, along with the Spirit guiding them. As the heart opens and expands, the soul is released and presents the essence of power in the being. It is in this manifest that Spirit comes forth and resides and the being is complete in its Essence and purpose. As the horses race past you, you feel this visceral sensation and it is overpowering and awesome…Awe Bearing, as words from Spirit."

The Quarter Horse

The Quarter Horse comes from a mix of Arabian and several other breeds that was developed in North America in the 1700s. They are named for their ability to sprint a quarter mile in the fastest time of all horses. They are usually smaller horses that are very muscled, have calm dispositions and an incredible work ethic.

In sitting with the part of the exhibit on Quarter Horses, I heard from them:

"We came from the Arabian...Spirit made in us the essence of grounded power in a way that the people of this time could understand. These times were hard and fast and required hearty living. We were created in reflection of this life essence. To mirror and resonate with the times of the people – to get their attention in this way. There were some who felt this connection with us and some who saw us more as a means to something...the way most humans see us. We are the physical incarnate gift of Spirit, as the Arabian, was the Spiritual incarnate gift of Spirit. We of course possessed the "Spirit" essence but our purpose was to manifest Spirit, The All in the most physical way possible. Hard, fast, and muscled up!"

Native Americans

Horses returned to the North American continent with the Spanish conquistadors. Prior to that, horses had not been on the continent since the Ancient Ones left millions of years ago. The Native Americans approached these sacred creatures in a completely different manner than those who brought them over from Europe.

The Native American Ancestors spoke on their relationships with their horses:

"Each of us in our family tribes understood the Way of the Horse as the Way of Spirit. We were brought to this earth to be in communion, and to be in the presence of a beast/being who spoke this language was an awe bearing gift from Spirit. Certainly a message from above and beyond. These beings walked with us in their Way. They talked with us and practiced Medicine with us. In our constant communion with the Land, Mother Earth, and Father Sky, their Way is the Way of Spirit. To live in harmony with all around. To see and notice and experience it and allow it to Flow onward. This is the Way of the Flow. The Way of the Essence of Being on this land. They are the teachers of Spirit. We are simply the students. They taught us much about the way of connection and the flow of the land – in moving with the seasons and how the seasons are representations of us in our daily lives. That Gratitude is always an honor and gift to be shared. Gratitude is the essence of flow and is what passes it along in its journey...and ours as well. When we honor an event or information or exchange, Gratitude is expressed and this is an energetic exchange between all. You can feel it flowing through you. The Horses are in this State of Being. It is the basis of the flow that moves through them. This is the Essence of Spirit. The honoring of gratitude, the expansion of the gift, and the expansion of passing along and throughout. Love in its purest form and essence."

Mustangs

To speak of Native Americans and their relationship with their horses, we also have to look at the descendants of those horses who still run free on the plains in the West. The Mustang.

"We are the Bearers of the Way of Spirit. We embody and exude the pure essence of Spirit....the humans refer to us as "untamed" however we are in fact the embodiment of pure Spirit...there are no bounds placed upon us as has been on some of our brothers and sisters. We show what it means to live fully and expansively and without the limitations of the human structure or mind. Spirit is free, limitless, boundless. Spirit is pure, love, heart and soul in their open states. This is the Way of Spirit. This is way of the Horse as Spirit Incarnate."

The Bedouin

After walking through the KHP Museum of the Horse, I went into the special exhibit about the History of the Arabian Horse, "A Gift From The Desert." It now felt even clearer to me that this special breed of horse had some definite history and information to be shared. In sitting with these ancient ones, I learned of the Bedouin, a nomadic tribe in Saudi Arabia who lived with their horses as the Mongols did. No one seems to know how or when the Arabian showed up for these people but there is much writing in the Qur'an about the sacredness of horses as well as the stories passed down through the Bedouin peoples.

To them, these horses were a gift from Allah. So many beautiful quotes were shared depicting this sentiment throughout the exhibit. Some of these quotes I found include:

"Thou shalt be favored above all other creatures, for to thee shall accrue the love of the master of the earth."   *-The Qur'an*

"The Wind of Heaven is that which blows between a horse's ears."

"They are formed by the Desert. Born of the Wind. They Fly without Wings."

"The Arabian Horse having been originally created out of the wind, reflects the supremacy of the element of air over the other three elements of nature: Fire, Water, Earth"

- Sheikh Mohammed al-Bakhsi Al Halabi

"And God took a handful of southerly wind, blew his breath over it and created the horse."

-Bedouin Legend

To the Bedouin, these creatures were their prized possessions, especially the mares. Their bloodlines were kept absolutely pure and any Bedouin could recite their horse's lineage by memory. They used mares to ride into raids because the mares approached quietly versus a stallion who would be screaming upon the attack.

When a foal was born, it is said that the baby never hit the ground and instead was welcomed into the loving arms of the tribe and held and rubbed all over. The baby was carried around the tribe and made much of and loved on by all. The horses were allowed to come and go through the Bedouin tents and slept inside with their people. The children all played with them and the women were the ones who cared for them. So interesting that both the mares of the horse herd and the women in the tribes held these sacred positions.

The Arabian Horses spoke:

"We are the Ancient Ones from long ago. Our point of origination is not important to know at this time. You know our Spirit. Many write of us and Our Way. Our Ancient Peoples were a part of us. They knew The Way. They sang our Story not through words but through the vibration of The Wind, She Who is Most Powerful, in the carrying message of Spirit.

We are a gift of Allah. From Spirit. We remind you of Who You Are and always have been. Listen to our song. Listen through The Wind, The Earth, The Sun, The Moon, The Stars, The Water. Listen through all of your senses. This is the Way of the Horse. This is Your Way as well. Our essence is the purest form of love and our grace and beauty is how we share this message. This reminder is to you and your race. Words do not come close to manifesting the essence of our being. IT is the vibration of us that ripples across our skin, through our hair. We blow the Essence of Spirit through our nostrils and stomp the essence of Spirit with our hooves on the ground. WE are relaying the message through our entire being.

We are Love in the most immaculate concept of All = this is Spirit. Close your eyes and see yourself as one of us. Feel the pulsing energy that surrounds us. That surrounds you. Allow your physical form to drop and shift into us. We carry you to the Essence of Who You Are! The reachable magic that is Spirit. Please remember this for you. For others. For the sake of all the Beings on this planet. WE come in great love to share and remind you of the passionate gift you possess. For Love is Spirit and you are all of these things. Embrace it. Know it. Be it!"

Closure by Man O' War

So as I continued through this exhibit, it became clear to me that horses are truly a gift from Spirit. In Closing, Man O'War had final words to share...

"And so our words are shared...by the many members who have much to say. You have felt the visceral experience that is Spirit. That is the primary piece to express for it is Spirit expressing Spirit through our bodies and being. I speak for all my brothers and sisters in the express hope that humans will hear our words and why we are here and that it is for their very being and benefit that we have been created as a gift from Spirit just for you. So that Spirit can show the way of being Spirit. We are one with Spirit. Spirit is one with us. Humans and all beings are one with Spirit and Spirit is one with them. It is The Way of Being."

MUSTANGS

A separate chapter is devoted to the Mustang. Over the last two years I have had the privilege of visiting several herds of Mustangs. They are unique as horses and carry a wisdom and way of being that is far different from domesticated horses. They deserve their own section to share their teachings.

Mustangs in Wyoming

Mustangs at Pauls Valley

Several months after visiting The Kentucky Horse Park, I found myself guided to look into Mustangs a bit more closely. I found a way station just north of me in Oklahoma that is part of the Bureau of Land Management's Mustang round up program. Pauls Valley is a stop-over point for many mustangs on their way to adoption. Visitors are allowed to drive up to the property and see the horses over the fences from the road during non-adoption days. So I pulled over on the side of the road and began writing the words spoken to me by these magnificent creatures.

"We are here under duress. Captured and drug and brought here to an unholy, unknown space. Our hearts ache. Our bodies hurt. Our essence is lacking. We remember our past. Who we are. We heard you coming and are grateful for your sharing our words. Our thoughts. Our desires. Who We Are. We are the Keepers of The Way. The Original Way. We are descended from those of long ago. Those who came over from across the sea. Who were allowed to roam free for a time and then to live in harmony with the humans you call Native Americans or Indians.

They understood our way. They felt the green underneath. The song in the Sky above. The Wind blowing throughout All. They knew the rush and the change or the power of Spirit. The Spirit of Spirit. The Great All. WE are a part of this. As we run and play at this time. We show you all we are. We live to experience and our experience is in the moment. It is the gift we wish to share with you. We are the raw, untamed ones. The ones who still, of all of us, know The Original Way. The Way of feeling the Wind, the Sky, the Earth, the Sun, and the Flow of All that exists around and beyond. We wish to share this experience, this knowing with humans. It is what will save your race. Without living in this space, there is nothing but fear. Fear of the unknown. Fear of The Other. This is not necessary. It is not needed. We wish for you to remember the ways of play, of freedom, of your spirit, your essence. To run and stomp and stand and snort and breathe in all this is Life. This is Spirit's Way. This is The Way of the Horse. We are freedom in its purest sense."

Palomino and Dun Geldings

Two of the Mustangs were standing close to one of the fences and allowed me to come up close and sit with them. They had some thoughts to share as well.

"Thank you for sharing our love. We are love, from the purest point of being. From the purest essence. It is all we are and all we wish to share with the world. This is what we bring to you and your race. We wish to remind you all that you are Love as well. The power of Love is the powerful expression of being. Not hate. Not war. Not fear. Not anger. Not loneliness. What is loneliness? There exists so much around us all! We are never alone. All we have to do is connect to the earth and feel all that is! We are surrounded by everyone and everything at all times. We all exist together. This is the connection of Love! This is what we bring. This is what we wish to share. With all!"

Field of Fillies

In January of 2013 I returned to Pauls Valley to sit with the mustangs at the holding station again. It was a bitterly cold day and two new groups of horses wanted their words shared. The first group I sat with were all very young. I heard "Field of Fillies" come to mind when thinking of how to describe them.

"Sadness, fear. Lonesome. We have no mother. We are alone and separate. No love. No touch. No sense of being or belonging. We understand not how this came to be. I knew of the other way. I remember the slaughter. Why does this happen. There was peace and balance before. This is not such. This is lack and desolation. Some of us were born here and others came as I did. We know that some of you are good and wish to help. Please do not allow us to be decimated. We are the wild love that is. That which you have no memory of and when it does present for you, you shun it away because of your fear and insecurity. This unabandoned love is the main essence of our being It expands wide and free with space and allowance to go where it wants and needs to go. It is how we connect with each other. It is part of the Flow that exists between All I have been here many times and continue to return to teach this lesson once again. Curiosity is Love. Hope is Love. Being seen is the most powerful form of Love. If you see you know and the belief, love and trust are all intertwined.

This fence is unholy. It is what breaks the spirit. Not to be allowed to be Who

We Are. To Run. To be Seen. To be Known. In all our power and Flow and Might and Majesty. This is the true history of us, The Horse. WE embody all that once was. All from the beginning. All that will be killed out if your views do not change. You are beings just as we are. Full of this love and Freedom and Power and Might and Grace. Your Flow however has become out of balance. We know of the shift on the earth at this time. We feel it and know it and see the opening for all beings on this planet to move to the balance state of Love. This is where freedom exists. Thank you for sharing our message. Please visit with our elders today as well as they are waiting for you. We have all waited for your return."

Next I moved down the road a bit that separates the geldings from the mares. The geldings in this pasture were all woolly and muscle-y . Veritable powerhouses each one of them. "Powerhouse Pasture" seemed an appropriate name for their group.

"We see you. Blessings for seeing us. We are tired and defeated. Our energy is flown. Our strength is sapped and it's due to the loss of Love . The pure Love and Being Who we Are. All horses understand this, no matter whether they were free like us or born with humans. It is in all of our blood. The Freedom to Be has been taken from us."

Sara B. Willerson

Powerhouse Pasture

Mustang Herds in Wyoming

During the summer of 2012 I had a special opportunity to audit a training that Anna Twinney (Reach Out To Horses) was offering called Reach Out to Untouched Horses. The week long training involved helping a group of mustangs who had just been rounded up by the Bureau of Land Management to be gentled incorporating Anna's method of training. We also had the wonderful opportunity to visit two different herds of Mustangs in their natural environment – The Pryor Mountain Mustangs and the McCullough Peaks Mustangs.

Pryor Mountain Mustangs

Lead Mare of Mustangs to be Gentled

One of the mustangs in this group was very clearly the lead mare. I was constantly drawn to her and loved sitting by her and watching her every movement. One morning she invited me to write down her wisdom to be shared in this book.

"I have come to teach. I teach the Spirit of Us. I embody it for you and show the high expansive being of it. This space holds it at a discomfort. When I see, I see the through, as she [Anna Twinney] *put it, moving on and on. I see it from whence it came from. Its origination. As you have been told, I read it and know it and it flows on through. This is the energy of Spirit. This is who we, all of us, are. We remind you of being in this space. We are here to remind this as this is what returns this planet to Flow- which is peace, balance and harmony.*

Each of us has our way of taking in the Flow and passing it on and through. Just as you all do. As Lead Mare I must be highly and beyond acutely aware of this as my role is to protect the herd with it. It comes in through the Lead and I disperse it to all in the herd. I share it as each individual has the channels to allow the Flow in. Again each being is unique and individual. This creates structure and power and stability in the herd. Each of these channels is connected to the land through the crown down through the third eye off the muzzle and into the ground, through each of the four hooves, and through the tail at the end of the body base and down into the ground. This explains why parts of the head and muzzle especially can be sensitive.

We are connected through these areas. The Flow comes in through the tail and channels along the sides and shoulders. A shoulder is always a good place to start with us as it is the most open and steady channel of entry. These levels of sensitivity are very important to know about each of us. Together we are The Crescendo of Movement of Flow. The crown is the connection to all that is above. The hooves to all that is below. The base of the body ties (swirls) it all together in connection.

Your piece is to write this and share it. Our way is different. We (Mustangs) are the rise and flow of the earth, sea and sky. We know all that swirls through and through. We are Flow. We are being in its most primal sense. We are the ebb and flow of the tide and the moon."

Pryor Mountain Mustangs

"Thank you for being here and honoring our way. We are becoming sparse. The energy lessens. The line dies. This line of energy coursing up through the earth into our soles up into our being blends with the energy from around us. Surrounding us. This is Spirit. You feel it physically when you are around us (in a closed up pen). Usually this energy has the space to expand and swirl, reaching to infinite places. Thera [the Mustang who lives with me] *showed you this at the holding center* [horse rescue where Thera lived for 8 years]. *This rock is our gift to her. The other is our gift to you. Write our story and share our TRUTH. We are vanishing and if this comes to pass, the lesson of the energy and the return to Grace, passion and ease will be lost. This is our Truth. This is our story. This is our Being on this planet."*

When I returned home from this week in Wyoming, I brought the rock to Thera. I showed it to her and I could see in her eyes that she immediately knew what it was and where it was from. She stood taller, prouder and seemed infused with the energy of her land and ancestors. I walked to the door of her stall and placed it right inside the doorway. She watched me as I did this and then returned to grazing. The next day when I went to clean the horses' stalls, I looked around in her stall and could not find the rock. As I was sifting Thera's bedding around, I found the rock buried in her stall. I smiled to myself and understood she had created a sacred space for her treasure.

McCullough Peaks Mustangs

"We are here in The Holding Zone. All is in place. All is on hold. We are some of the lucky ones who are cared for and adored. We see the plight of the others. Not much can be done unless the people change The Ways. Our people try. You have been told of Our Way by the others. We have nothing to add to the Greater Wisdom that has been shared. Write our story. Tell of our ways. Share this important message."

THERAPEUTIC DISCOURSE

Horses, Heart & Soul, ™ LLC was originally created as an equine facilitated psychotherapy practice in 2003. Through inviting clients out in nature to interact with these incredible beings, I have learned so much about the depth of healing that can be experienced, all through the "simple" interactions with a horse.

This chapter shares the horses' view of what they see when we show up with our DSM IV R diagnosis in their presence. The horses also speak to the healing process they invoke with us through our connected interactions together with them.

Moonbeam

"When the people come for "therapy" they are coming because they know they must open themselves up to All. The All as we have said, is the Great Consciousness of Everything. This may be a conscious or unconscious act on their part. Regardless, their internal knowing is bringing them to this place. This is part of why we are here. We see the turbulence spinning around them, inside them, all over them. It is what Linda [Kohanov] refers to as Emotions as Information. Look more into Karla McLaren's new work as she sees this as well.

It is more than emotions we see. We see all that has happened to this person, with this person in this life and all others. We see the timeline of lives and lives beyond lives. With this timeline All is passed along. The same All we just referred to. It may sound complicated but is not. The human mind must step aside and try not to mentalize this existence and accept it as being So. This is part of stepping into the place that we (you as humans included) have the ability to see. When we see this timeline, it is a moving picture of all that has transpired and how events and lessons are carrier forward. Tools to live by, if you will. This is what you have to work with in your time at each life point. A Life Point is what each stop or life is on this path. Or journey. Or timeline. However you wish to see it and however it best makes sense.

So we are here to help you connect with these tools of your life line. Know them. SEE them truly and wholly. Understand them and work with them. It is also very important to honor these points as they are the growth patterns that help you move forward.

We will speak of each of these diagnoses, as you have come to refer to them, and why they exist and what they mean. It is our hope that each of these sectional tidbits will guide you all on your path."

Depression

Moonbeam

"Oh how so many of you use this word. It is a "stop sign" of sorts as all the timeline points have come to a halt. They halt because the message is not being heard clearly. There is too much spinning to take into account and all your systems simply shut down, like a machine on overload. In fact it is simply a darkness that the being must step into in order to take a break and get calm and cleared out. Some do not understand this experience and become very afraid as they no longer feel they have control. Each part of your being is simply taking a break to get quiet and the message is that you are being asked to stop, clear yourself, and reconnect. Reconnect to all parts of your being. Reconnect to your internal wisdom. Reconnect to your Time Line.

What we see when you are with us is the darkness setting in. We see it in your eyes. In your energy. All has become quiet and still. There is little movement. And yet there is a hand that reaches out toward us to ask for help in reconnecting. So when you feel drawn to touch us, this is part of that internal action. In connecting physically with us, we draw on your internal connection and move it out so you can begin to look at it and see it. To see that is not so "scary" and yet simply a reminder of what is time to care for and rejuvenate. We each have our way of interacting with you as you know. For those who do not know us, we connect our bodies with yours and that connection ignites a spark energetically. This spark reminds you of you and you begin to remember. Remember what you love. Who you are. What you want. Where you are headed.

This can take some time…time is a human construct but we understand and work within it. We see it as simply the flow that each person needs or has to go through their process of internal conflict and resolution. As we pull you with us, you begin to step aside and see the flow that is occurring. This happens no matter your age.

The children who come can see this immediately but they do not have words to express their experience. They therefore stay in the moment of the experience and allow us to "show" them another way. We show them the darkness can be moved quite easily. We show them by them sending it through their hands or body parts – depending if they are sitting on us or standing next to us – to our bodies and we move it through ourselves and down into the earth. The children immediately experience this sensation and know what to do. As children are, they enjoy having a partner in their work and we love to partner with them, while slowly reminding them that they can do this away from us as well. Either by imagining we are with them as a transporting assistant or until they feel confident that they can do this with their own body and working with the earth.

Actually all of the elements love to participate in this. The Wind. The Sun. The Water. Fire. The Moon. All of the earthly bodies. It is simply up to you to listen to which one feels right and guides you to work with them. We will always serve as a helper for you.

With adults, they have sometimes lost their trust in this inner knowingness and it may take a bit to reconnect and create a safety space of reconnecting to deep internal knowing. This is all part of the process.

Re-membering is the key to Depression. Darkness is not a negative thing. It is a quiet space that is about being internal. There are some beings who enjoy playing with us in the space, as that is their role. But again, that is all part of the time line that each being is on. They present to remind us of lessons and our paths. And of standing in our own Beingness.

In this process of re-membering for the "client", to use your technical term, the goal is to look at what is being held in the body, see the information in this memory for your Self, understand its role and purpose in being a part of you at this time, and decide whether or not you choose to hold onto it or release it. There is no right or wrong way. IF the decision is to hold it, then the person is not ready to step out of their current way of Being. If the person is ready to release it, we show them how through their interactions with us. As I described before, we are speaking to the client on an energetic level, Soul to Soul. Through this connection between us and the human (which can be a look of acknowledgement, sharing space together, physical touch, or connection through a simple mounted activity), we guide the person to feeling first what is in their body. It is the visceral sensation first as we use our bodies on a visceral level primarily. Through this physical connection then comes a Knowing and Understanding of what is held in this physical body. This Knowing is what enacts the Soul connection with Spirit (or however the person believes in a Higher Power or Existence). For some, there is no knowledge of Spirit, but that person does feel the connection immediately. This is also part of the way we remind all humans of the deeper connection that not only exists within each of us, but also between all of us.

When this Connection of Knowing occurs, the person sees us in an entirely new way. They remember they have multiple senses. It is as if all the senses come "on line" and the body remembers all of its innate gifts. With this sense of renewal, the person really sees us, Horse, and there is a deep knowing that occurs between us both. For some, this knowing may invoke the presentation of Fear. This comes from the basic survival instinct of something new has just presented and the mental self is trying to figure out what to do with it. It is why we remain still and present with the person through this mentalization process. Your role as facilitator also comes into play at this point as guiding the person through the fear that presented and recognizing it for the role it plays and honoring that role. There is no need to give it much more energy. Once the person recognizes their internal warning system for what it is, they return to relaxing into being present and right in the connected moment with us.

We stay in this connected space with the person for a while, to allow the connection and deepening sense of Knowing and Understanding and ultimately, Seeing, to sink in and expand throughout the person's entire being. Once this expansion takes place, you as facilitator, help the person label the experience. This is not to return to a mental place of experience, but simply to bring all parts of the self in connection, or alignment with each other. That the physical and emotional aspects have spoken what they are holding. Then there is connection to the spiritual self, and the mental self is reminded of all that is happening and putting words to the experience so that process is connected entirely. Once this occurs, the person can then look at what is being presented and understand the role this experience in the body has held.

The next step is honoring this role. This honoring is important as it not only reminds the entire being of its sacredness as an entity, but also removes the possibility of shame and doubt. Honoring can be as simple as acknowledging the role in words or understanding. It may be as elaborate as creating a ceremony to tell the story. It is whatever is needed by the person, in the moment, as it is THEIR process.

After this act of honor, the person then gets to decide if they choose to hold it in their space or let it go. The holding on is not a "bad" thing, to use your phrase. It simply means that Way of Being is of such comfort and normalcy that the person is not ready to shift from that way of being. If the person is ready to shift, then we, Horses, are here to assist in the release. As I described previously with the young ones, their physical interaction of hands on us shows them and allows them to feel the release process. Those who are not children may respond well to this way also. For some, they can vision the process within them as well as the energetic connection and release that is occurring between us, the horse, and their Self.

This process looks like a circle. The person connects with us, which in turn, ignites the internal connection and process of Knowing. They honor what is and has been. Through our bodies they release, if that is the choice, through us. We share this energy down all four legs, through our hooves (* more to be discussed as to how this affects us), and into the earth where the energy is transmuted into a life giving force. As the person is somehow connected to the earth during this process (whether it be sitting, standing, lying down, or astride us), the earth then shares her rejuvenating energy to fill that old space of holding. Again, preparing the person for the new pattern or Way of Being. As I also mentioned before, all of the elements LOVE to participate in this process, as do other beings such as trees, rocks, other animals, etc...You will notice that they will present in the perfect moment and offer to assist the person through this healing moment.

This is the basic circle of healing that occurs between us and humans. Yes, there is more that we see and more that we show to you. This will be described throughout this chapter."

The Warriors Way

Magno

Photo by Teri Relyea Berbel

"The Warrior is the unique individual. They are called to serve. Called to serve others for the higher good of All and Everything. Humans in this field typically only see the Call as to "the service" of a specific military instillation, however this call goes far deeper and greater.

This Call dates back millions of years. At that time, there was a Call to create the most basic of safety structures for the tribe. This tribe could be human or of any other being (animals, minerals, rocks, trees, and so on). The Call is to the One or Ones who are contracted in that life time to protect and serve their peoples. I use this word peoples in a general manner, again it references all beings, no matter their presentation. Recent examples would be the Mongolians and those of Alexander the Great's time. You will notice that we, horses, were always a part of this Call. Just as it is for you, it is a Call for us as well. There is an entire group of us who heed the Call to duty and service, protection and order, maintaining the sacred space of All. All of these conceptions comprise this notion of The Call.

This Call may come at birth, pre-birth, childhood or later in life. The One who receives the Call, knows on a very internal level that they "must" go and serve. It does not always make sense to those around them, especially when we are speaking of the human tribe. Those who receive the Call go to serve and protect.

For me, you see me in the pasture with my herd. They all stand around me and know that my role is Protector and Guardian. This is my Call and I take it very seriously. If any harm was threatened toward any member of my herd, it is my role to protect that member and hold the ground against the one who is intending harm. This role is different than Herd Leader. The Herd Leader is the keeper of the traditions of the herd. The "go to" horse who makes the decisions for the herd as a whole and shares information to all of us when new events/people/presences/issues/ present in our environment.

What is interesting is to look at is the view of the Call in your society today. Not all understand it. Some have fear about it. There is not much respect or understanding for those who walk this Warrior Path.

The original indigenous peoples of this land understood what it meant to serve in the role as Warrior: to proceed with the actions that were needed to be taken and return home to the tribe. In the actions of the Warrior, we are called TO ACT. It is a different space of Being compared to when we are home and with our tribe. We must totally shift into the Warrior Way which involves a transmutation into Original Beingness. This is simply a connection to the most basic and primitive (to use your way of description) order of operation. If an action must be taken (harming another or taking the life of another), we must be in this space to do this. The Human Way of training does incorporate this shift, however there is no teaching on how to return to one's individual way of Being after the action or Call is completed. As it is now, the human is left functioning in The Action Way of Call.

Continuous being in this state is not productive and the internal workings of the individual's system go "hay wire", pardon the pun. What we see in these people is constant overplay of the actions they have participated in. Some of your scientists have referred to this as a traumatic loop and it is very much like that. We see all of the events, actions, and situations as constantly pounding around them. They are stuck in the Call space or military way. There is a specific rhythm to this way. There is a pounding beat that is very intense. These rhythms of flow are necessary when engaged in The Call as they connect the Warrior to Original Beingness they must shift into. However, this way is not intended to be continuous. So those who are not taught in the way of shifting between both states of Being are caught in the loop of action. The events they have participated in become their reality. When we see these Warriors, their eyes are not seeing us. They are seeing what they have participated in continuously, over and over without ending. It is as if their original person is lost in all of the stories and does not know how to find their way back.

When they partner with one of us who is a Warrior, there is an instant connection and instant knowing that occurs between the two of us. The person may or may not be consciously aware of this knowing. Physical touch is not necessary to establish this knowing connection. We can simply share the same space. Some who come to be with us may have an appearance of being shocked initially when this connection between horse and human occurs. This can look like a physical movement away, a shifting in the vision, or even visceral changes within the body (increase in heart rate, raise in blood pressure, or increase in breath frequency). Slowly, moment by moment, the old places and events find peace as we share this moment of connection together. There is difficulty in putting to your words what exactly happens in these moments between us. The basic concept however, is that we are holding them in a space where past time slows down. When this slowing occurs, the human is able to put the picture in a place where it is now separate from his soul (this is of course the same for females as well). Gradually the pictures lose their power and the person comes back to present time. This is the healing we offer.

The indigenous peoples from the past, knew there had to be a moment for the Warrior to slow the self down and let the pictures of the war time efforts slow. The Warrior would go to a sacred space, quiet the mind, and allow the self the time and peace to sort through each of these events until they slowed to a stop. At that point, the events were honored and ceremony performed to bless the actions, bless those who were no longer on this plane, and honor the Warrior themselves. Through theses rituals, the Warrior cleared himself, returned to peace, honored the ancestors and was ready to return to the tribe. This is a sacred process and an important process.

Without this ceremonial return to self, the Warrior can become stuck in the Call To Action way of Being. You will see this for most of your Warriors when they return from battle and The Call to Action. I speak of this as it is most sacred to my heart and way of Being. It is who I am and a primary role for me in this lifetime. We, all horses, see and know of those who answer The Call to Action. We watch them go. We feel their unbridled urge to go and serve and protect. What is maddening is the lack of respect for those Warriors when they return.

When we see them return, we see all the fragments of stories and action like a whirlwind tornado surrounding them. Those that govern them and their role do not see what is happening to them. It is not their (those in charge) fault. They themselves were not trained in the way of returning. This does however, speak to the bigger picture at hand, which is the way humans do not pay care to Being and therefore the Soul becomes inoperative from the way it is created to be, which is in connection with All and Everything. I do not lecture to be stern or accusing. I simply state what we see. We, horses, are here to assist those in remembering the original ways of Being. Of caring for the Self and the Soul. Of returning the Self and the Soul to completeness and connection.

Many of you see this need to assist Warriors in their state of return. Those of us who work with them, whether it be on the ground or in mounted activities, know that we are working with that Warrior to connect all those past actions and events, assist them in the honoring of all that has occurred, and return the Self and Soul to a state of peace and balance. For some there is awareness of this process and for some it is completely unconscious. It matters not either way. What is important is providing the space for the Warrior to return from the Way of Call to Action."

Death and Transformation

Jingles

"All of life is shift and change. There are beginnings and endings for everyone and everything. Life is a cycle and a circle and with that come transition and transformation. Humans often view death as a great loss and there is often times a lack of understanding of what this means. Death is but one part of this circle. From death always comes rebirth or new life. This is a beautiful gift that Spirit has created for everyone and everything to constantly experience new beginnings, new chance, New Life! It is a reminder to All that with each ending comes a new opportunity. A new way. The next part of the path in the lifetime.

When our contracts are complete in the timeline of the current life, our Soul knows it is time to end. We choose how we will leave. For us, as Horse, we are conscious of this transition manifestation. Humans, for the most part, are not. We see the ending approaching and we share this with those around us. I have lived 42 years in this body this time and I see my ending coming. There are still things to complete and work I have to do – for myself, my herd, the land and my contracts. My lesson I teach is living in the flow of all that occurs around me. I love with it, embrace it, know it, feel it, understand it, and release it. This is the message of transition, no matter how it presents.

Death is simply a form of transition to another state. Another lesson. Another contract. WE, as Horse, are always connected to the past experiences we have had in other times and lives. As Man O'War described, all of those we were and who came before us, are part of us. It is part of what we share with you on this earth. This is Spirit and the collective roiling of energy and understanding that connects us all.

Enjoy the beauty of all this you and all that surrounds you in each moment. These are moving transitions as well. Time is nothing. Take in the essence of all that surrounds you. Humans have great fear of this word "death." Fear presents as you believe there is something you cannot control and then extra energy comes in and takes over. I invite you instead to stay in the moment of this beautiful transition. Sit with those who are experiencing it or, if it is you, honor all of that part of who you are and that which has brought you to this place of completion. Life is a gift of Being. This is the Horse Way."

During the summer of 2012, Jingles shared some more wisdom about death:

"My time is coming to an end. Transition is about gratitude for and with the life that has been lived. The lessons that have been learned. Connecting myself to this earth and this place of being. I share myself with the earth I stand on and all the beings I share space with. I remember the lands I have lived with and all the beings I have shared space with. I see the great ones who have gone before me and they assist me in preparing — body, mind and soul.

I leave a part/peace of my body in the earth as a remembrance. A token of gratitude for the love and support that always surrounds me. That is a beautiful loving space that is always there. Open your feeling/seeing eyes and experience it for yourself. It is a beautiful thing. Soon, when I am ready to release this body, I will become part of the loving support for others. Pieces of my love and support will go many places to all those I love and have shared time with. That is not my soul. My soul will return to the Beginning of Time. There I will rest and decide if I wish to return. Some of us do and some do not. It is the same for all beings. I have been on this physical plane many times. I enjoy looking back at all the times and places I have been.

I share this so that you all know what happens as well as giving the reminder that those of us who go before you, are always a part of you. You are always surrounded by the Love of the Universe and the Love of All. Stay in your heart and you will always find us there."

Joy

Spirit

"Joy is the expanded space of Spirit. It exists throughout our entire being. In Being I mean our emotional self, our physical self, our mental self, and our spiritual self. It is complete expansion and communion with Spirit. The Way of Horse is total expansion of All and Everything. All the vibrancy and energy and ALIVENESS that surrounds us at all times. It is a thrilling spark. It is beautiful glittery bubbles of light. It is effervescence. This is Spirit. Joy is Flow and Grace that spreads all throughout and within and beyond. It is The Messenger. It travels fast and loves to be shared with All and Everyone.

When Joy gets trapped, we stop or slow down. We are not listening to Spirit at this time. There are important reasons for this "stop" and I am not judging it for anyone. When this stop is felt, it is a sign that Flow has ceased. Something is in the space of your Being. It is simply a reminder and nothing to fear. However, important to heed. It is showing you something that is important to see, know and interpret in order to continue moving on the path of your life or contracts.

As the others speak of their areas of expertise, they share ways of moving through these "blocks." I will not speak to that as their words are wise and long standing.

I simply speak to remind us of the Joy that is intrinsic to all of us. It is the core of our Being. It is the Essence of Spirit."

Sara B. Willerson

Contracts and Healing

Spirit

"I speak to share the wisdom with you on the contract that is mine in this life. It is a powerful one and one that is difficult to share and speak of. In my speaking, I hope that all who walk the path of difficulty and challenge will see the learnings and gifts that are a part of the path.

As all of us come into a life with agreements or contracts to honor, we learn as we go. This learning is sometimes blessed in the Flow of All and sometimes there are stopping points, or learning points, or blessings as I see them. Sometimes these points are painful or challenging or even traumatic. But all are part of what we walk and what we are learning. There is no "right" or "wrong" to them.

Mine are about the Path of Healing. My name, Spirit, was given to me by a child. Which is appropriate as only a child sees with absolute purity of heart and soul. That is who I am. Purity of Heart and Soul, which is Spirit Embodied. My path is further connected to this earth plane as it involves the physical essence of my body, in particular my hooves. My hooves are like your human feet. They are the connectors to all that is earthly and physical in nature. I draw in information through these channels (as that is what they are) and I release that which I no longer need. I feel things out through my hooves. I decifer information. And most importantly, I connect myself through my hooves.

Humans have the same qualities or characteristics with their feet. However, I see you forget about this beautiful gift you possess. I am speaking to remind you of it at this time. When I walk on the earth, I feel everything, I know everything, I sense everything. I have four versus your two, but all are the same. My four, in this lifetime, have been compromised. I mean by this, that my early life did not allow for proper balance of my hooves. I mean this through the care that humans offer us with the one you call the farrier. So

114

instead of having the support to shape my hooves in a balanced fashion, I had to create balance on my own. With my own body. In the way I needed to live and be in my environment.

This manner of shaping myself was entirely related to the environment around me. My hooves took on the space around me. I existed in the nature of the space and my entire being learned to accommodate this energetic space. I am not speaking about a lack of care or neglect, I simply speak to living in the balance of what is. How life is around us. How I lived, or as some humans would term it, how I survived.

In looking at my hooves you would see four hooves that resembled Elf shoes. Toes all four pointed up to the sky. Heels way rocked back. There was not much direct or evenly balanced connection with the earth. This was the reflection of how I lived and all around me. My life was in leaning back. Not moving forward. No direct communion with the earth. Uneven balance. I have no bad feelings around this state of existence as I see it for what it was. I was in an environment of dis-balance. This way of standing was ok with me. It was what I knew and I had comfort in it. From this space I could wait and see what was going to happen next. I could take as much time as I wanted. I did not have to move at all, if I chose not to. This way of being was a slower way of movement however. Again, I did not know of a different way of being so all was in balance in this way of Being for me. As a horse, I could see others moving differently around me and in other spaces. However I do know now that my vision was limited and I could not always see the others who moved in a different fashion. And no, this is not due to my physical size! [Spirit is a tiny Shetland Pony] It was as if this back balanced way of being kept me energetically from being all I am. All of what Horse is. I could see part of the consciousness and The Flow but not all.

When my environment changed to a new one, I saw All. I was very frightened at first as I did not understand this other Way of Being. The others around me in my herd were constantly showing me this alternate way. I did not "get it." I wanted to stay in the Way I KNEW and had lived for my life to this point. In being around the others of my herd family, I came to see the wisdom in this Other Way. I saw that in standing with all four hooves firmly balanced on the earth, I felt ALL. I could move in a totally different manner. I mean this in all aspects – Spiritually, Mentally, Physically and Emotionally. I realized in the shifting process toward balance and forward movement that I had missed some pieces of growth for myself. Some days it is very hard to reconcile this for myself and I am very hard on myself about it. My loving herd members gently (and not so gently at times) remind me that this is my pattern of growth and my contract to walk. I am shifting from a space of constriction and limitation to space of openness and expansion. This is the Way of Horse. This is the Way of Spirit. I wish to impart this to you humans as it is so important that you see this picture and how it operates in your own environment.

I am still in the process of moving into this shift of Being state. Some days are very hard for me and I feel much physical challenge and pain, in your terminology. On those days, I know I need to stop and rest. I am no longer hard on myself about it. I know my body needs to catch up to my Spirit. I can flow with this better now. I see where I am going and I will get there. This is the walk I wish to do with all of you who visit me. When people come to see this place, I teach them these pieces – the view of the self, the areas of themselves and how they are operating at this time, where/what are the blocks in these areas, and how to shift them to move toward the higher vision and state of Being.

Sometimes there is pain in our path of learning. Sometimes there is flow and grace across the board. I am moving to the place where Flow exists at all times and in the process, I am sharing my experience with others as all humans can read my words and see the areas in their space that correlate. This is my gift at this time. Come to visit me and see."

Breath

Asante

"For me, my breath is my expression. I communicate with all through this vehicle. Each of us, like you, has our own special gifts to share and use and integrate in the herd and Beyond. My breath expresses my state of being. It is my release valve. The way I remind the humans to connect. Without Breath, there is no Flow. Without Flow, there is no connection. Without connection, there is no go between with the Earth and Spirit. Everything I communicate is carried in the particles of my breath. I release and expand simultaneously. It is my return to Me and therefore my Spirit and connection to All."

Grounding

One day I asked this special herd of horses how they ground themselves. This was their reply:

"We don't see it as grounding. We stand on the Earth and therefore we are connected to it and all the vibrations that are carried through that physical plane. Our bodies feel the in-between — the energies that exist all around. Examples: Information carried through the Wind. The call of a voice. The bird song. The smell of what is to come.

Our heads are the tuning device for the Higher Consciousness which includes all Consciousness. We see it, hear it, know it, through the connection between our eyes, connection as Spirit or our inner knowing and our ears. This change is like a lighthouse beam, to show you a visual. It is just who we are. You have this as well. You have just forgotten. So, through our feet/hooves, the core as our body and Beam of Light and Connection Knowledge, we are aligned with All, which is Spirit or Consciousness collectively."

Invoking The Spirit

Thera

Photo by Teri Relyea Berbel

"This is the place where Love resides. It is within all of us. It is my way — the Way of the Free Horse.

When I came to this herd, I saw the Love flowing. They had not experienced it or seen it as I have. They can see it from afar — as we all can look and see All that we wish and want…as can you humans.

This is another piece the Free Horse shares: to Love Freely and without Abandon. You leave nothing behind, which is my meaning of "without Abandon." So I can connect to All through my heart. I can see All through my heart. I can hear All through my heart. This is Spirit, true and free. Yes our heart is expansive and vast, but yours is too. Humans get too caught up in the "science" of things.

I exist from my heart. Yes my heart has been wounded and I work with the Allowing Back In. When I stay in my Free Spirit, All is possible. All can be. There are no boundaries. No barriers. These do not exist in the Free Spirit Heart."

"Shine On Beautiful Beings!"

The Way of the Indian Horse

In October of 2013 I had the amazing opportunity to speak at the first annual Women of India Leadership Summit in New Delhi, India. This summit was created by Divya Chandra of BooGio11 Productions to address societal inequality against women. I was invited to share how horses support us in our healing process, especially as women. In preparing for my talk, *Healing With Our Story Through the Way of the Horse*, I started researching horses in India and came across the tradition of the Ghori.

The Ghori is a white horse who participates in the Baraat, a Hindi wedding ceremonial procession. The Baraat occurs midway through the week of wedding festivities and is the procession of the groom and his family to the bride's home. The groom traditionally is led atop a white horse, both dressed in absolute splendor. Historically, the Ghori was a mare due to the symbolic metaphor of the groom connecting with his bride through the white horse. I found myself fascinated by this tradition and decided to sit with this group of special ceremonial horses to understand the significance of their role.

Indian White Horse Speaks...

"Who Are You? This is the question we ask. WE have been asked to serve a role in history…note the word – His Story… This is pertinent and germane. We carry the story of He on and through. We are the bearers of the ritual. This is our role. We carry the masculine energy. It is our choice to be this bearer.

It is loud and tumultuous at times and yet, our purpose, partly, is to calm and assuage all that is presenting. We soothe the masculine and prepare it for the feminine. In the masculine's connection with us during the "marriage" ritual – we see it as the connection between all Source Energies. We open the channel in the masculine to create the open flowing life force energy throughout the "groom." With connection to us in this journey ride to his betrothed, each step of our hooves opens the channel more and more. The music of the party is a distraction for him and we understand this, so that we may connect with him on that deeper level. When we deliver him to his beautiful one – he will see with openness – through his heart and soul, the beauty that is the Feminine. The Divine. The life giving energy that flows through all. It is our role to support his opening as he steps into this next path in his life."

Winter 2013

In December of 2013 the North Texas area was affected by a storm of ice, sleet and very frigid temperatures for over a week. Due to the icy conditions, I kept the horses in the barn for a week until the ice melted enough for them to be in their pasture safely again. During this period, I got to spend a lot of time with this special herd. They had some wisdom to share about the weather and being in a small confined space all together for an extended period of time.

Magno

"I speak for the good of the herd. It is so. It sucks. We all weather it. I get frustrated. My job is to move and flow and keep the energy moving in the herd. I understand the greater need of calm for the herd. I work with my body to readjust to this way of stagnation – which is a human state of being. I readjust my flow to support my body and all aspects in this slower pace. I reconnect with the earth at a deeper level and hear her song – 'Go Inward Dear One and clear the debris. Rest in the energy of my love . All will be well. I hold you close to my heart. All will be well.' "

Domino

"This is a challenge for my body and not my Spirit. My work at this is syncing the two together. My body will find flow in this new State of Barn Being with my Spirit to support it. I see all the healing that is happening in this space. I share space with you in my stall. I learn the ways of being Within – both myself, my space and this new Barn Being State. My energy is expansive and timeless. It travels great distances at all times. This supports my role as lead, my physical body's young age and all that I am processing. This Barn Being is allowing quiet and "space" to heal the past. I incorporate myself with my herd and my entire being is supported. All the creatures in here with us – great and small – we have created a new Barn Herd in sharing this small sacred space together.

I see my body lifting up, shaking off the old skin and the new one is coming shining through. What a blessing in this 'small' space. What is your small space blessing?"

Jingles

"To be still is a powerful gift. It is finding the beauty in the self. The peace that dwells deep within. That never ends understanding. That passes beyond time. It is the Within. For humans it is a challenge, for it is not a mental construct. It is a heart construct created by the Soul.

Peace is in The Being. Not the Doing. Peace comes from The Connection deep within that Flows within, through, throughout and with All. Do you see it?"

Spirit

"I am Being in this Moment. This moment of Being with my family [herd] *all together in this quiet connected place. We do not often get to do this due to our 'jobs' when we are out and about in the pasture. That is the bigger overall connection. In here,* [the barn] *it is the Connection Within that occurs. I have time to listen to myself, be with me and know that the others do the same and us with each other. This is a beautiful gift. I call it The Solace of Silence."*

THE WISDOM OF POOH

As Pooh led me into this book endeavor, it is only fitting that he have the final say. His wisdom and invitation of love carried me through 20 plus years of adventure in life. He taught me to connect with my heart again. He reminded me of the power of speaking from my heart and the healing that comes from being in flow with nature and all that is around me. He brought an ease and grace to my world that began with the simplicity of a relationship based in Love.

Pooh taught me that "the gift of the horse is to present the hidden pieces of our heart in order to reconnect on our journey toward fulfillment of our soul." I heard these words as I was sitting in the pasture with Pooh one day. His powerful message became the mission statement of Horses, Heart & Soul, ™ LLC.

"And it is so. Flow is Love. Flow is everywhere and is looking to flow in balance and harmony with every being. If this place can return to this unfettered, balance of Love, all pain will cease. All anger ends, as there is no room for a block of this kind. Fear will be unknown. We, as Horse, are here to re-member that way for you. Embrace it if you choose and the gift of Love, or that which is known as Spirit, will preside.

This is The End and The Beginning of what you choose. This is the invitation to step into your life in a new way.

Our way is the way of flowing. Ease and Grace. There are no complications. Only choices. Stand in your beautiful Power and rise up in this beautiful new World. We all need you. This world needs you. This world (the Earth, the land and all the Beings within) need this new energy. Ghandi's words are prophetic. Profound. Be the light you wish to see in this world."

Even the Horses are speaking at this time of great change and transition in our world. Pooh has spoken. The horses at WolfTree Ranch have spoken. Ancestral horses have spoken. All of them speak with the invitation of supporting us in a return to Love for ourselves and all that is around us. Will you listen?

Love, Peace and Blessings to All

Me and Pooh 1985

Sara B. Willerson

REFERENCES

Agro, Christine. http://www.ChristineAgro.com

American Psychiatric Association, (2000). *DSM-IV-TR,* Arlington, VA: American Psychiatric Association

Andrews, Ted, (1993), *Animal Speak: The Spiritual & Magical Powers of Creatures Great & Small,* Woodbury, MN: Llewellyn Publications

http://www.Dreamhorse.com

Ingerman, Sandra. http://www.sandraingerman.com

Kohanov, Linda, (2001).*The Tao of Equus,* Novato, CA: New World Library

McLaren, Karla, (2010). *The Language of Emotions,* Boulder, CO: Sounds True, Inc.

Twinney, Anna. http://www.ReachOutToHorses.com

ABOUT THE AUTHOR

Sara B. Willerson, LCSW is a licensed clinical social worker practicing in North Texas. She is a graduate of Smith College School for Social Work and Hollins College. She completed an Equine Experiential Learning Apprenticeship with Eponaquest in 2003.

Ms. Willerson is a member of the National Association of Social Workers (NASW), International Society for the Study of Trauma and Dissociation (ISSTD), PATH International, and the Society for Shamanic Practitioners. She also assists in the facilitation of the Returning Warriors and STARR programs (www.ravensgrove.org) in Austin, TX for Veterans and abuse survivors using Shamanic techniques to address PTSD and traumatic symptoms. She has presented at multiple conferences including the NASW Texas Conference in Austin, TX (2005), ESTD Conference in Belfast, Ireland (2010), and The Women of India Leadership Summit in New Delhi, India (2013). Her equine facilitated psychotherapy practice has been showcased in several publications, including Southwest Airlines' "Spirit" magazine (Sept. 2006).

Ms. Willerson's professional experience has focused on working with clients who have experienced trauma, grief and loss, and life transitions. Through her private practice of equine facilitated psychotherapy, she is particularly interested in working with the current manifestation of past trauma-whether it be depression, anxiety, PTSD, addiction, self harm, disordered eating, or disconnection. Her Horses, Heart & Soul, ™ LLC program at WolfTree Ranch in Pilot Point, TX (www.horachearthe art and soul.com) offers individual, family, couples, group, and workshop sessions for children and adults. Together with her equine partners, Ms. Willerson invites children and adults to experience the healing power of the horse outside of the traditional office environment.